PANTHER
TO
PRIESTHOOD

EDDIE LEROY WILLIS

DESERET
BOOK

Image credits:
Pages 30 and 103: childhood images courtesy of the author. Page 62: photo by
Chicago Sun-Times Collection/Chicago History Museum/Getty Images.

DESERET BOOK is a registered trademark of Deseret Book Company.

Visit us at deseretbook.com

Library of Congress Cataloging-in-Publication Data

(CIP data on file)
ISBN 978-1-63993-020-3

Printed in the United States of America
Lake Book Manufacturing, Inc., Melrose Park, IL

10 9 8 7 6 5 4 3 2 1

I don't know of any person of **PREFACE**
African descent who hasn't had to
deal with race—especially Blacks in America. I am part of that
category. Though my challenges have been great, it must be said
that everyone has challenges they must deal with, overcome, and
hopefully get through. Our lives are not only about just going
through things, even though it may sometimes seem that way.
Life is about purpose. Purpose can be found in family, friends,
neighbors, or society. From a young age, I wanted to find purpose in life.

In all my years as a youth, as far back as I can remember, I
never felt that I had very much worth. Even though I was made
to go to church—and there were many churches to choose
from—I never felt or understood that church was a place where
I could find value in myself. I did not understand that I had
worth to Heavenly Father or that I had value through Jesus
Christ. I did not understand that I could have the kind of relationship with Heavenly Father and the Lord Jesus Christ that
would surpass the value that many place on people or things.

Before I found meaning in those eternal relationships,

PREFACE

joining the Black Panther Party[1] was one way I found meaning
and value and grew educationally. I was able to learn the history
of people of African descent in this country, which gave me
some dignity and some self-respect. That kind of information
had not been available in the schools I went to. It certainly was
not available in the media. Still, it took me many trials and trib-
ulations in life to finally get to a place where God led me to The
Church of Jesus Christ of Latter-day Saints. Though I had always enjoyed popularity within my social circles and purpose in
various endeavors, until finding the gospel of Jesus Christ, I was
never satisfied in my quest to understand my worth. I believed
and knew that something was missing.

Everyone is looking for the love that they need. Part of our
responsibility as disciples of Christ is to be people of value and
help to others. We must do something outside of ourselves and
break through life's challenges in order to fulfill our true poten-
tial and help others to fulfill theirs. Everyone has a story. Many
people within my race may have a story that is similar to mine.
Many must still deal with the disparity between those who have
access to a better life and those who do not. Some struggle with
terrible burdens and believe there is no one they can call upon
for help. But there is nothing too high, too low, too wide, too
strong, or too impossible for the Lord.

Nothing surpasses the love of God, and it is our duty to do

1. The Black Panther Party was a political movement founded by African
American college students dedicated to advocating for the rights and well-
being of Black Americans. Active from the late 1960s to early 1980s, the
party was well known for their somewhat radical fight against police brutality and governmental persecution, which involved heavily arming themselves and dressing in black leather and black berets. The party also pursued
initiatives to support Black communities, children, and families, such as
providing free breakfast programs, educational resources, and medical access to African Americans.

the best we can to emulate the Savior's message of love toward our fellow men, no matter their race, creed, or anything else. During these troubling times, as in times gone by, there have been conflicts between fathers and sons, brothers and sisters, and so on. After a life of searching for answers, I found a source of peace that could surpass all of the conflict within myself as well as within the world. I hope to share my experiences so that people may know and understand that God is full of love, mercy, and grace. God is waiting to hear from those who can and will feel the Spirit and will hear His voice when He calls. No matter who you are in this life, what you've done in this life, or what ethnicity you are, you can call on God with repentance in your heart. He will not hesitate to move heaven or hell to rescue you. I am the proof.

PROLOGUE

It was racism, yes! We all knew that the white folks around us hated Black folks. We knew it. And they knew that we knew it. They may not have said it to your face—they never do. But we all knew how they felt. We Negroes were the problem. The leeches. The welfare queens and the deadbeat dads. We knew about the projects, the redlines, the sellouts. We knew it was the truth.

But was it the truth? Or was it all about money? I knew poor white folks too, and they didn't seem so bad. They seemed to know a little of *the struggle*. The wealthy folks just wanted to keep us from rising up against them. Was that it? Perhaps it was. But . . . it wasn't. The obstacles, structures, and barriers were crystal clear, apparent for all to see. And I needed to stop *being* history and start—to the best of my ability—making it. I had to find my place in the world and my reason for being here.

Stories about Black folks are hard to tell. We tell stories about our skin, our bones, our blood, and our flesh. We tell stories to each other, to our kids, and to our enemies. When we're at family barbecues, at church meetings, or in the living room, we understand each other intuitively. There's a shorthand that we all just get. No dictionary necessary.

But when the white folks enter the room, things change. Translating the Black experience for white folks doesn't come easily. Living in our skin, in our bones, with our eyes, and with our backstory? There isn't a crash course available at Barnes and Noble called *Being Black: White Folks' Edition*. But that doesn't mean we don't have a story to share. I'm going to try to share mine.

I was born in the frontier of America: Oakland, California. On the frontier, we define ourselves, redefine ourselves, and free ourselves. In our frontier, we lived under the cloud of a national history, one built into the roads, the warehouses, and the police departments. Choices, we had. But the future haunted us when the lights over the city went low, when the coke-smoking, heroin-using addict sat or stood on the corner.

We know—or we *think* we know—my ancestors' story.

Hauled from their home in West Africa and thrown in ships like cattle, they had to redefine themselves. White folks decided where, how, and whether they would sleep. I knew little about my ancestors' lives.

But one thing I *do* know: in the Latter-day Saint faith, we sing a song about how pioneer children sang as they walked. Well, my ancestors sang as they worked—at whip and rifle's end. When my ancestors were freed, the same men who had run the cotton fields now stood over them as they "freely labored" on the same plantations where they had lived for years, under the same whips. Pregnant mothers were seen as part beast and part profit. When ordering the women to receive a lashing, the overseers wanted to protect the unborn slave child they saw as their future property. So, they dug holes for the pregnant mothers to lie in, stomach down, to ensure that the hurricane of blows did not touch the child.

Even at their most barbaric, white folks knew that they needed us. So they did not destroy us. No—they did not want to eliminate us. We were too important, too valuable to them. The women of our communities were their nannies. We were their porters, their shoe shiners. And they knew that we had everything we needed to become their competitors. Control, watch, bind, manipulate, and when possible, exploit—that's how the white folks did things. Every once in a while, they managed to get a few Black folks to back them up. Give them a white shirt, a bow tie, some glasses, and some lighter skin? They got along just fine.

∎ ∎ ∎ ∎ ∎ ∎ ∎

I grew up in the slums. The promise of America was on the other side of town. Not my Oakland. Their Oakland. Their city.

3

Their rules. The city managers tried to sell Oakland to America as "The Bright Side of the Bay." For us? It was Dog Town. Ghost Town and the Lower Bottom. When folks go to developing areas and comment on how happy the poor people are because they "just don't know any better," they're fooling themselves. People know they're poor. We knew we were poor. We knew that being Black in America came at a price.

This was not a place where sane people would choose to live. To the social workers, we were "cokeland." To the politicians, we were welfare parasites. Housing developers thought we were a threat to their way of life, but I never felt like a threat. I was just a kid rolling a tire. I lived in a city of shadows. We were the part of Oakland that "respectable" folks liked to pretend didn't exist. We were an embarrassment. Sometimes, we think of the 1950s as a pleasant time, a time with *Leave It to Beaver*, with *Father Knows Best*, and with the antics of a good-hearted Dick Van Dyke on television. But that wasn't our time.

Father did his best. He wanted to be one of them: a civil engineer, they called it. He always had his nose in a book of some kind. He wanted to build a city to make our homes better. Anyone could see that the folks running the show seemed more interested in making a world fit for the white folks than for us. But Dad was a dreamer. Everyone thought Dad was a real somebody. He was a porter on the train, so he got to go places and see things. Chicago, Seattle—cities that seemed better off than our slums. But Dad was on foreign territory, *their* territory. He could never be welcomed there. Dad knew a secret. He knew that Black folks couldn't just talk however they liked. If you spoke too well, enunciated too clearly, you'd be branded an "uppity n*****" faster than you could say "ghetto."

And yet there was an irony in all of this: the white folks were foreigners here too. The city managers, the lawyers, the bureau-crats, the health inspectors—they looked over the slums with a kind of paternal eye, making sure that we kept up—and were kept out. So, our time was a time when TV families became weapons to remind us of who we weren't. Everyone knew that television's "reality" was not our reality. Everyone knew that be-ing Black meant you were poor. It meant being broken, being homeless, and walking with bullseyes on our heads and backs. The world we lived in was not of our making. We knew that. The white folks knew that. Everyone knew that we were living in a phantasm of a world made for us.

I cannot claim a corner on growing up in hard circumstances. Brothers and sisters in Appalachia live without running water, good education, or easy access to food. Friends living on Native American reservations struggle with rampant drug addiction, poor housing, and dirty water. I was lucky. I had a mother, and sometimes a father. In Oakland, the ghetto alienated us. Forgotten men became hardened men. You survive an atrocity or two, and you wonder what the point of it all is. West Oakland wasn't the place you lived to find yourself. In West Oakland, if we wanted to survive, we figured out friend from foe. If you didn't, you were dead. Life on the streets placed me on the edge of suffering.

A cloud hung over West Oakland: tuberculosis. Black folks have long been susceptible to this disease. The white doctors called it the "Negro disease" or the "Black disease." It had more to do with substandard housing and resources than skin color, but it didn't matter to them.

All I knew was that I was sick, and that I was about to be locked up with a bunch of other sick kids. We were sent to where the other Black kids were suffering. It all felt like one more tool in the grand plan to keep Black folks in their place.

Where did we go? To the Livermore Quarantine Facility. Only a few years earlier, they had kept the Japanese here during the war. I suppose we were in good company. Being a Black child with TB meant you were a prisoner-of-war in the clutches of an invisible enemy that, as usual, hung over our community. Being Black with TB meant you lived in your room alone—not even your parents could talk to you or come near you. There was a small window they could peek through to see me, their small, Black-bodied, suffering child.

"What do you want, child?" they would ask me.

"I want to go home," I replied. But they were not able to fulfill that desire. My second request was to have a guitar. My mother came back with a small plastic guitar with rubber bands to resemble strings. The following day, my father brought me a guitar bigger than me—of course, I was happy with the bigger and better gift. I would attempt to play it standing up. Though I inquired about why my parents were coming separately, no answer was given. Later, I found out that they had separated. As I went through life, I often wondered: *if I hadn't gone to the hospital, would we have made it as a family?* Even as a young child, I had questions about my place in the world and about families.

I looked around and saw kids going through worse. One little boy bled out his nose without warning. He wiped his nose, smearing the blood on the blanket. Another cried and wailed while snot flowed from his nose. One child seemed to have the devil in him. White folks thought we Black folks were diseased beasts. But no, the problem was that we lived in a world made for beasts.

Life in quarantine meant a life where you made your own meaning. God wasn't around much when I was a small child. We

7

weren't exactly churchgoing Blacks. We were survival Blacks. We did what it took to make it to the next day.

When my release day came, I saw my mother and another man, a man she called John. We lived by an alley near where John worked. My time in the medical brig needed to be kept quiet. A TB child was a shunned child. Whenever I tried to learn about what had happened to me, Mother lied to me. "You had a spot on your lung," she told me, changing the subject. Why was she so quiet about it? How shameful it must have been. And *how Black*.

. . . .

I hated hearing the N-word. Every time. Especially from my own. After the age of five, I had recovered from the Black curse of tuberculosis and was doing what all the other kids did: using nothing to create something fun, even though it still looked like nothing to everyone else. In my case, it was rolling a tire. And John didn't like it.

"Get over here," said John, swearing at me and calling me that hated word. He sat on a bench with this kind of snarl plastered across his face. He always seemed to have it. He tossed his whiskey bottle in the garbage can and walked my way.

"You little . . ." He let out a string of expletives. Pardon the language, but this was my world as I saw, heard, and felt it. You'd wonder what a little boy like me could do to get a grown man to speak like that. Not much. I had rolled a tire around when he didn't want me to. But John had a tough life. He was the sort of man who had a grin as wide as the Mississippi and a temper twice as powerful. I'd see him sitting on the corner bench, swigging a mouthful of liquor in the middle of the day. He had work, but he never made very much. So he and his buddies would sit by the cheap church on the corner across the street from us and talk about how horrible we kids were, how poor our neighbor was. On no point was he wrong.

Before I could make my escape, John had turned me upside down and unleashed a hurricane of blows. John was a mean man. He didn't like kids. He certainly didn't like me. He didn't like life. Little work, no future. He picked up a board lying in the street and unleashed his fury. He couldn't talk very well—he was so soused. But what he couldn't say, the board sure did. Blacks in my neighborhood had no problem giving other Blacks a whooping if they felt a mind to. But drunk men exhaust quickly, so he put me down and told me to get back to my affairs.

It wasn't about me. He didn't care about me. He lived in a world with an uncontrollable past and an uncertain future. He might've thought it was something I did—that I was a petulant child who needed to learn a lesson. And maybe I did. But poor men are frustrated, tired, and silenced men. Poor men are emaciated, emasculated, and stifled men. Stripped of their power to determine their own destiny, they compel others to accept their own version of the world: hard, cruel, and heartless. John wanted people to know that the world had been unkind to him and that these were the rules he knew. Some folks' destinies are a little harder to come by than others. And my destiny would be the same as John's if I didn't find some way to change it.

■ ■ ■ ■ ■ ■ ■

In our Oakland, talk of "community" was talk for people of means and standing, with their spectacles and bow ties. They sat in their air-conditioned offices, talking about "the Negroes" and their problems and their community leaders. But there in 1950s Oakland we had no Dr. King. We had no Malcolm X. We, the children, weren't souls, but "problems." And in their minds, we were problems of our own making. Meanwhile, the city council sent health inspectors, bulldozers, and bureaucrats to condemn our homes. They came up with all kinds of initiatives: "redevelopment," they liked to call it. "Urban renewal," they said. Their policies and programs would help us, they promised us. James Baldwin, an American novelist and activist, called it "Negro removal."

Maybe they meant well. But what it looked like was serial eviction from our homes. Oakland was too run-down, too poor. So the better idea was to kick us Black folks out of our homes and let middle-class (white) professionals move in. While the white men played around with their maps and their numbers in their offices, we Black children played with our tires in the streets. They had the bird's-eye view, but we saw the streets.

"Neighborhood improvement associations" popped up all over in an effort to prevent Blacks from moving into white neighborhoods. The white organizations with money made no secret about what they wanted: the eviction of "undesirables" and the creation of restrictive agreements through organization of block-by-block anti-Negro contracts. When you had people who looked white and had money fighting you, it was a tough gig for a Black person.

But my mom managed to get by. White people liked my mother. She was their kind of Black. "Nothin' but a house n*****," the other Blacks would say. We knew how to be racist too—even against our own people. Had "good hair"? You'd get a little more respect. Lighter skin? Love and adoration. Other

Black people would always act on their best behavior around us. My mother exuded the beauty of a Creole goddess. Fair, slim, and confident, she spoke her mind to all she met. Some Black folks liked her in front of her face, but not behind her back. She was pretty and pleasant with white folks.

And that's how things were for us. We weren't so fooled as to think that we could dominate our world, conquer it, or control it. We Black folks didn't really believe things had changed all that much since our people had been freed. We still cleaned white folks' businesses, washed their cars, served their food, and made them wealthy. Black folks worked and served.

■ ■ ■ ■ ■ ■ ■

But we always needed money. Survival meant you worked with folks you didn't like. One day, John and my mother called me to the table. They had an opportunity, and I could help. It sounded exciting and new—better than rolling around tires and being beaten for it. So we boarded a bus along with some other Black folks and Mexicans, riding all the way through the night.

By sunrise, we had arrived at the land of promise . . . a cotton field in Bakersfield. I remembered the stories Mama had told us about Black people being slaves, cleaning white stalls, washing white clothes, making white food—and picking that cotton. And here we were—voluntarily picking cotton, probably for more white folks.

"Do I gotta pick cotton?" I asked my mother.

"Yes, if you want to get paid," she replied.

I liked getting money, so I got in line. We were handed some burlap sacks, and then we wandered out into the fields and did what Black folks had done for a very long time. No one talked.

11

There was no singing or laughing as we fingered the soft, raw crop. What I saw was a group of brown-colored folks working in a field with a white man watching them. If a guy wanted money, he had to get it from the white man, arms folded, looking down on the Black folks toiling over King Cotton.

A few drips of sweat became a torrent. I looked over at my mother. Her back bowed, she picked the cotton with a special kind of fervor. In cotton remained her hope, her dreams. Not for life—just for the next few days. That's how we colored folks had to see things. I earned $1.50 that day.

Some folks say that the poor are lazy and uncreative. Not our poor. No opportunity was beneath us to earn a few bucks. We did all kinds of things to pay rent for our rat-infested hole. Mother and John even turned our home into a chicken butchery. Crate after crate of chickens met their untimely fate within our humble abode.

∎ ∎ ∎ ∎ ∎ ∎ ∎

We kids had our fictions we lived by to deal with our realities. I was always looking for an escape, for something better. We played cowboys and Indians and pretended like we were army infantrymen. I loved to put on my cowboy hat and saunter out into the street with my guns in their holsters. I always wanted to be the good guy, the protector of the weak. Big piles of dirt at a construction site were perfect as our homespun reinforced fortifications. Good and evil, justice and injustice. I was a believer that it had to be out there. I dreamed of one day finding it.

We played on streets with debris littered all around. Poverty, crime, and violence lurked in the air. No matter. We went about our day, enjoying the fantasy that we made for ourselves.

Donning my best John Wayne outfit, I bickered with my buddies over some injustice. Dressed to the nines in my perfect cowboy attire, I watched two drunk Black men argue near the wall of the corner store. One of the men staggered into the street, pulled out his gun, and fired without a word. The other man fell. Our Oakland.

Mother swept me into the house. The shooter? He was too drunk to run, preferring to stand over the body, the gun still in hand. His fate? Who knows? The adults kept asking us, "Think the cops care when one of us kills another?" White folks didn't care who killed us, as long as we were handled. Even as a child, I knew that the whites could kill me or hang me and go free. A corpse now rested in the street. An old homeless man walked by, looked at the dead man's face, and walked by.

I turned to look at the hollow storefronts on the corner. Had something changed? Not particularly. The same waters ran into the gutters. The same people milled about, going in and out of the shops. Things were as they always had been. The blood had flowed away. The muggy air continued to suffocate us.

The white folks didn't like to trouble themselves with the mess of our streets. It was a long while before the police and the ambulance came to take away the body. It just lay there in the heat. The police didn't seem interested in conducting interviews, getting information, or establishing the truth. They threw the shooter in the back seat and drove off. This was just how Black folks died in our Oakland.

Even though all of this was how things were, my mom never taught me to be prejudiced against whites. She never expressed hate or acted as if this was the end of our road. She helped me to believe there were better things ahead for me, and I truly believed it.

Mother was a believer—not only in God, but in the **3**
Dream. Anyone with two bits of sense wondered what
kind of God could be at the wheel in our neighborhood. But once I got old enough to go, mother dressed me in
an old bow tie, suspenders, and slacks, and sent me down to a
broken-down church sandwiched between the liquor store and
the whorehouse. As far as I knew, if I was going to have a future,
I needed to go to that church, the one that I heard reeked of
bad perfume and liquor.

There were lots of churches in West Oakland, but even they
felt stripped of spirit. The sacred had no place in my Oakland.
There was only power and bread. But I liked to look inside the
churches. Something drew me to them. I wondered what things
were like there. Did they sing about love? Jesus? Family? A small
placard with the words "Christ's Apostolic Ministry" scrawled
in someone's best effort at handwriting invited folks to come
inside. But in my West Oakland, it looked like Jesus had better
things to do than look after the antics of a bunch of Black folks.

But Mother—she was a believer. "You behave yourself," she
said.

"Will do, ma'am," I said.

I strolled down the street to the church. You could see the shooting site from the corner. "Come on in," the pastor said. He was kind enough, but this wasn't my turf. All these adults in nice clothing (nicer than mine, at least). Me, with my shoddy clothes? I looked like an orphan. "Don't be shy now, son." I took my place in the circle formed in the center of the room. We joined hands in a circle and began to sing "Onward, Christian Soldiers." These people seemed so kind. And I felt so bored. The song was slow, ordinary. I began counting the moths I saw hovering around the dim lights above. But this was God, Ma said. So God I would seek. God in the ghetto.

How could a little boy consider the transcendental when he knew that anyone—white or Black—could take him out at any moment? Could there really be a divine being in the same space with shootings, robberies, and drugs flowing freely?

After several weeks of attending the church on the corner, my mother informed me that I was to follow everyone to a larger building with more people. Here, they had a system. They threw us kids into a room and told us to get dressed in Sunday clothes. Most kids didn't seem to have a problem with undressing in front of others, but I did. Ma had taught me about modesty and decorum, even if we were poor. Our clothes may not have been nice, but when you were around others, you wore them.

So I sat down and waited. Then a big woman came bounding into the room and demanding that I change. She pulled my clothes off and forced me into a white uniform. I looked around and the other kids were getting in line—all wearing the same clothes. We were all lining up . . . for *something*.

"Where are we going?" I asked.

"Come along, Ed!" the lady exclaimed.

A shout and a scream pierced the silence of the room where I was waiting. The large Black lady was leading us to our deaths! This was it. I knew Mama felt frustrated that I didn't brush my teeth or comb my hair, but I didn't think that I should die for it. "Please," I begged the woman, "let me live." She rolled her eyes. *And what was that smell?* I finally met my fate: a large pool of water with a Black man in a white coat, smiling. *Who are these people?* Surely, Mother knew better than to leave me in the hands of a white-coated beast. I squared my shoulders and walked toward the grinning, white-coated man.

After saying a few fancy words, he pushed me under the water and pulled me back up again, so quickly I almost took in a lungful of water. As I gasped for air, the crowd cheered and spoke in an unknown tongue I couldn't understand. That was scary! I suppose I had been a good boy, and I lived to tell the story. Mother even hugged me and told me I was good. I was told I was now a Christian. It would be years before I gained a full understanding of what that name could really mean.

I didn't have many friends in the Lower Bottom, my neighborhood. I did have three that I favored, though. One was Eddie Wright, who was two years older than I was but just as poor. Anthony was my age. His family owned the store on the corner. There was also Terry, whose family owned the store across from the cleaners we lived behind. Eddie was Black, Anthony was Mexican, and Terry was white. My mom would always let me take Eddie with us when we would go on trips to the country for big picnics or barbecues. Eddie was a very good fighter, and other kids would steer clear of me when he was around. Anthony and I played cowboys and Indians a lot together, and his mother and father would always give me treats. I never saw him play with any other kids in the neighborhood. Terry's mom would give Terry and me doughnuts and sodas after our outside play, and I was also allowed in their home to watch cartoons with him.

In my early age, race was very confusing. The last six months of my quarantine in the hospital, I'd had a white nurse who had treated me with tender loving care, but when the shift would change, I had a Black nurse who would treat me roughly. Terry and his mom never seemed to act as if I was any different than they were, but I didn't see them treat any other Black kids like me. Excluding my mother and father, all other Black folks would indicate that whites hated us. Both of my friends' families' stores would give my mother credit without hesitation, which most other Black families couldn't get. Needless to say, this would cause me problems with the other kids and led to fights.

■ ■ ■ ■ ■ ■ ■

On one particular day, I had made my rounds with all three of my friends, ending with Terry. While his mother was giving me a treat, one kid came into the store and told me that my mother had been calling me. So Terry's mom told me to hurry home. Upon approaching our house, I saw my mother talking to a lady I had never seen before. My mother said, "Eddie, this is your grandmother." The lady gave me a big hug and a kiss with a smile.

"How are you, Little Eddie? It's so wonderful to see you, son. I am your father's mother," she said. She was so nice and sweet to me—of course she was my grandmother! It was a happy moment for me in the Lower Bottom, connecting with parts of my family I hadn't known, until my mother said, "Little Eddie, your father has been shot. But he lives."

I started to wonder more about my family. My ancestors had been in the area as long—and longer—than many of my white neighbors. They built America too. But the choice to contribute had not been theirs to make. They lived on farms owned by rich white folks, and they played by *their* rules. If we wanted to survive, then we worked the cotton fields, did our dance, and smiled big. And while that might spare us the lash, it wouldn't spare us the indignity of being forced to be two people: ourselves and the person white folks expected us to be. Black folks have long imagined the exodus, the escape. Back in the Jim Crow days of the South, our people left for the North to escape lynching, rape, and voter suppression. They turned Chicago, Detroit, Harlem, and Philadelphia into havens for Black life. Us? We just wanted to live away from the shadows, from the daily dose of what the ghetto had to serve up.

But no matter how hard we tried to get by or what age we were, kids needed men—fathers. We needed strength. My mother cared for me, watched after me, made sure that I did right by people. But there was something only Dad could give me. John couldn't. John was a no-goodnik of a man. There was no man there to push me up, only one to knock me down. He was frustrated, but so were we all.

■ ■ ■ ■ ■ ■ ■

My mother knew that more family would be good for me. Somehow, she convinced John to drive us to Galveston, Texas, to see my maternal grandmother along with our other relatives. I received so much attention! I really didn't understand all the fuss, but I enjoyed it. I liked the feeling of belonging to so many people who cared about me other than my mother. It was new for me. Two weeks in Texas was quite an experience. I had such a good time, but then it was time to go.

We did not leave until mid-afternoon. We said our good-byes with hugs and kisses and hit the road. We were all bubbling with conversation about meeting uncles and aunts and so many others. After traveling for hours on a naked road in Texas, the sudden sound of a siren frightened us.

I heard my mother ask John, "What's wrong?"

"I checked the car before we got under way," he replied. He had checked the car indeed—not just the brakes, oil, and gas, but the headlights and brake lights too. Everything quieted down quickly as we pulled over to the side of the road. We turned around in unison to see a police officer exit his vehicle with his hand on his gun. It seemed as if he were moving in slow motion. He stopped toward the rear of the car and stared at me in the back seat. As John rolled down the window, humidity filled the car, which only added to all of us sweating even more. I didn't understand what was going on, but I could tell that my mother and John were feeling abject fear. So was I. I knew if they were afraid, I had plenty of good reason to be afraid too. My mother looked back at me and whispered, "Be quiet, Eddie." I didn't say a word.

The policeman told John that he was speeding. John told the policeman that he was not speeding. However, the policeman would not accept his explanation. "You tryin' to sass me, boy?" he asked. "Give me your license!" he ordered. This made matters even tenser. John handed him the license. With that, the policeman walked back to his car and got on the radio. When he returned, he ordered John to get out of the car immediately. John began to exit the vehicle, but before he was all the way out, the policeman grabbed him by the arm and slammed him against the side of the car. "I will blow your head off, boy!" he yelled. John was soon handcuffed and placed in the back of the police car. The policeman began to drive away. He turned down a dirt road that led to a small house. There was nothing else around but my mother and me, left alone.

My mother seemed to be very anxious. However, through her worried face, she would look back at me and tell me that everything was going to be all right. I didn't believe it, and I didn't think she believed it either. It had been dusk when the police car had turned in toward the small house. When the side window of the house eventually lit up, my mother scooted over to the driver's seat and began to fumble with the keys in the ignition. I knew she was trying to decide whether to leave or to wait. It seemed that we sat there for hours. Finally, we saw the police car coming back in our direction. I noticed that my mother was extremely nervous. The police officer dropped John off at our car and said with a smile, "Y'all have a nice evening, you hear?"

That ended the joyful chatter about our visit to Texas. In fact, there was very little said for a long time—not until we got to Arizona. It's a good thing my mother had money, because they had made John give them all of his.

■ ■ ■ ■ ■ ■ ■

Just because the law tries to take us for a ride doesn't make us good or bad people. When I saw that police officer cart John off, I realized that getting manhandled by the law doesn't give us martyr points—it turns us into a statistic. Black victims of police brutality could be good people or bad people, nice people or mean people. They might be my friend, or they might want to punch me straight in the nose. But when they found themselves at the hands of yet one more incident, for a brief moment, we were brothers. I recognized the kind of life I needed to prepare myself for.

I remember a couple days after arriving home that John was sitting on the couch, watching TV. I had my toy gun handy, and I pointed it around. I liked the feel of it. I felt strong. Powerful.

"What you got, boy?" John asked.

"My gun," I responded.

"Let me see it!" he implored. *Why did he want my gun?* "I'm gonna teach you something about the world right now," he began. "Look at the television set," he told me. I looked. I saw a bunch of cowboys talking tough to each other. "Those guys? They're not your friends," he explained.

"What do you mean?" I asked.

"I mean, there's gonna come a time when you need to run from them. And you won't win. They'll win because they always win!" he instructed me.

"I thought they were the good guys," I said.

"Sure they are—for their own," John retorted.

I furrowed my brow. Mother walked into the room and John handed back the gun. They left for the store, leaving me alone with my thoughts. John's words would stay with me for years.

My mother had a dear friend named Henrietta who lived in a nice neighborhood in Berkeley, California. Berkeley had good streets with well-dressed folks. Mother liked to visit to take her mind off things and to forget our unimpressive apartment in the back of the cleaners on 34th and Hannah. When we went to visit, it seemed that Henrietta might as well have been in a different country. People didn't talk jive like we did in the Lower Bottom. The Black folks in Berkeley talked, dressed, and acted like the white folks. They played the game, and because of it, the respectable white folks humored them.

Once when we were visiting, I came inside from playing with Henrietta's kids and I heard my mother laughing. She hadn't laughed in a while. I peered around the corner, and my mother stood hand-to-mouth giggling like the girls in school do. Standing next to her was a tall, bulky man laughing with them.

"Little Eddie, this is Willie. Willie Thomas," my mother explained. Mother and Henrietta were readying dinner. Willie was a light-skinned Black man with wavy hair, and he didn't look, dress, or act like the other Blacks I knew in the Lower Bottom.

He dressed like the white folks. He wasn't talking jive either, but he had a deep Southern accent. He looked over his shoulder, watching all the fun going on outside.

"Are you Eddie?" he asked.

"Yes sir," I responded.

"Come on out, my boy. I've heard so many good things about you. Your mother tells me you're the best kickball player back in the whole neighborhood. Is that true?" he asked.

"I guess so," I said.

"How about we go outside and you show me how to do it right? I'm an old man who doesn't kick like he used to," Willie gestured. Willie grabbed the kickball, tossed it to me, and we went outside. Mother and Henrietta shooed us off.

We kicked the ball around for a few minutes. Mother then came outside and walked up to Willie. Out of the corner of my eye, I caught a glimpse of their fingers interlocking. I didn't let them see it, but I smiled. I liked Willie. I could tell that this was not their first encounter. As we were getting into our old car later, Willie kissed her. I hid my face—mostly. He went his way, and we went back to 34th and Hannah.

■ ■ ■ ■ ■ ■ ■

Most folks might want a dramatic story about an intervention, or someone stepping in to save me from John's rage. Maybe the police should've stepped in, or a friend could've stepped up. But as usual, it was my mother who saved me. We didn't need white police officers to save us from ourselves. One day, I returned home from school, not thinking about much. At our little shack on 34th and Hannah, I saw a big truck with men in uniform. Mom was directing affairs, and there was Willie carrying some boxes. I caught my mother's eye, and her face broke into a wide grin. She left the moving team, walked up to me, and grabbed me by the cheeks. "Little Eddie, we're getting out of here," she said.

"Really? Where are we going?" I asked.

"We're going to go to the East Side. We've got a lawn, and a home, and nice streets. We're going to live with your new daddy, Willie!" Willie then swept up behind me and tossed me in the air. I looked around. Was this what a family looked like? It was a small taste of a feeling I'd always longed for.

We moved to East Oakland, and it felt like a very happy time. There may not have been many faces like mine, but I was tired of all of the faces in the Lower Bottom. I wanted new faces. Different faces. In East Oakland, people seemed to be happy, and I wanted to be happy with them. I didn't see anyone getting shot there. There was no run-down storefront church. No John to wallop me. When people saw you in the streets, it didn't feel like they were going to hustle you, swindle you, or kill you. They smiled, because it was the nice thing to do.

Our home felt like a mansion. We had a kitchen made for the rich and famous (or so I thought). We had running water with pipes that didn't make loud banging noises, good knives and silverware, and even fresh vegetables. Outside, we watched some rich white kids go horseback riding down the street. The neighborhood kids were mostly white, but that felt just fine so far.

The other Black family in the neighborhood were the neighbors down the street. They had two sons and a daughter. The oldest son was named Sonny, who became a regular playmate during the summer. We played the same games and watched the same television shows. Sometimes, our white neighbors would host barbecues and invite us over to eat hot dogs and hamburgers. Oh, how good things were.

■ ■ ■ ■ ■ ■ ■

My new school was called Markham School, but with all these white faces, I wasn't sure how to feel or act. On the Lower Bottom, the streets have rules. What were the rules the white folks lived by? I found out eventually. Besides myself, Sonny, his brother and sister, and two others were the only Black kids in the school. The two others were siblings, and they were mixed.

Other than the occasional racial slur, the white kids didn't bother me much. But the mixed kids? The other kids wouldn't have it. They were called mulatto. Half-breed. Mule. Chocolate milk. And so on. If we Blacks stayed to ourselves—in our place—then we seemed to get by. But if a Black boy sidled up a little too close to a white girl? Race mixing came with a price. Boys and girls were competing for each other's attention. I wanted to impress a girl on the monkey bars. But then Kenny came. Kenny was a tough guy who also felt like he could charm all the girls. He had rolled-up sleeves, walking around thinking he was a real somebody. As he walked with his shoulders back, never exerting too much effort, most of the boys gave him a nod. Kenny ruled the show when the teachers weren't looking. And Kenny liked the same girl I did.

I dropped from the monkey bars when I felt a sharp push behind me. "Hey, n*****!" I knew that word. I had heard it in the Lower Bottom all the time. But here? Now? In this space? It became a different word. I whirled around and punched him in the face. Before he could punch back, the teacher on duty swept in and broke us apart. But Kenny cried and griped and pointed his finger at me while all the white kids watched. They watched, waiting to see what the little Black boy would do. The teacher believed Kenny, try as I did to tell her my story. It didn't do any good. "I will be telling your mother," the teacher sternly replied. She made me sit on the bench while Kenny went off to play with the other kids at recess.

When I got home, my mother was extremely angry and put me on punishment. My mother seemed to be embarrassed by my behavior. I didn't want to make things worse by trying to tell her that I felt outnumbered and alone at that school. Whenever I got into trouble at school, my mother would always tell me, "You go to school to get your lesson, not get in trouble."

In the days to follow, I wanted to eat lunch with the white kids. "Seat's taken," they all said. I wanted to play kickball with them too. "You can't! Go away!" they all replied.

One day, I wouldn't have any more of it. I grabbed the ball, yelling, "If I can't play, none of you can!"

Another mob of white kids formed. A little girl erupted into tears. "You dirty little Black boy. You think you can just come in and play with us, don't you?" she cried. I was done. White, Black, Lower Bottom, West Side, or East Side, it was all terrible. Black kids hated me in the Lower Bottom, white kids hated me on the East Side, and maybe I hated myself for all of it.

The problem didn't last long. The government decided that they needed to build a new road, and our house was in the way. So they bought out the community. I believe they called it "eminent domain." So when I was ten, we moved again. No more white people on horses. We were back on the West Side—exactly where the white folks wanted us to be.

1516 Linden Street in West Oakland was our new address. It was the summer of 1957, when I was ten, and I sat on the front stairs of this new roach-infested abode looking over the neighborhood. I witnessed two boys walking down the street in my direction. As they passed by, they began to giggle and laugh. They started hurling rocks at me. Without thinking, my response was to pick up rocks and run after them. My first thought was, *here we go again.*

It was a long summer without any friends, except there was this one pretty little Black girl named Wanda Williams who lived down the street. She was friendly toward me and had a pogo stick that she allowed me to play with. Little did I know when I met her just how special this pretty little girl would become in my life.

Life was still tough in West Oakland, and the only peace that I had was when I played with Wanda or when I went to the Antioch Baptist Church for Sunday school. None of the kids there were looking for a fight, but it didn't seem like anyone was looking for a friend, either.

Linden Street is where Willie, my new pops, gave me a whooping for the first time. Back then, whooping children was legal, and my whooping came because I busted another kid in the head with a brick after he lied about me to the meanest woman in the neighborhood. He would throw newspapers in her lovely flowerbed and then tell her I was the one who was responsible.

Needless to say, his mother was horrified by the brick incident. Blood was everywhere, so she called the police, who escorted me to our place. I knew both of my parents were at work. The police officer left me at home, got in his car, and drove off. I thought I had really dodged a bullet, but a nosy neighbor had seen what had happened. I was very nervous about what I had done, so I waited at the bottom stoop of our house until my pops got home. As he approached, the first thing I did was ask him: "What would you do to somebody who lied on you and got you in serious trouble?"

His reply was simply, "I'd kick their tail."

With that, I joyfully skipped on down the street thinking all was well—until I returned home. By then, our nosy neighbor had informed both my parents what had happened. I think my pops gave me a whipping because he felt that I was operating in deception when I had asked him that question earlier. He was correct.

All the challenges of my growing-up years caused anger and frustration to a degree I don't believe I understood as a child. The only way I knew how to express myself was through violence. As I understood it, my life had no value to whites, or to Blacks, or to my teachers. I knew my parents loved me, but they weren't going to be with me all my life. At some place and some time, I was going to have to be in charge of myself. I had no idea what God thought about me. I believed God couldn't have thought good of me, because I was always in some kind of trouble.

■ ■ ■ ■ ■ ■ ■

After some time, we moved to Berkeley, which I was already familiar with because of close family friends like Henrietta. Berkeley had no ghetto. This was very hard for me to believe, but it made me very happy.

Berkeley was a new frontier where all races lived among each other, and most people seemed friendly. I had some adjustment challenges because it was hard for me to trust such friendly behavior. My aggressiveness from grammar school followed me into junior high school, which is when I accidentally heard a conversation of some fellow students that gave me cause for concern. Their topic was *me*, and it wasn't pretty. To them, I was mean, violent, and too scary to be around or be friends with. That made me feel terrible, so I made a conscious decision to do better. However, doing better only meant that I adapted, not that I changed. In other words, the enemies inside me were still there.

One thing that really made a difference for a short while was when I became a silver certificate student, which meant I was a B-average student! In sixth grade, I started applying myself more in

Eddie at about age 14

30

math. Most of my problem seemed to be about just not caring. But when I saw how much it affected my mother, it helped me to want to do better. My mother had been very good in school, and once I started asking her for help, she did it in such a way that I enjoyed it. Some nights, she would have to get up and make me go to bed because I was up having fun with math problems.

Another positive during this time was that I began to excel in sports! I tried out for and made the baseball team first. But it was in track that I showed much promise. I was going to be a sprinter. This also led the coach to making me a wide receiver in football. All of us guys who played sports were friends, and we each had a girlfriend or a girl we liked. Our quarterback liked a girl named Wanda. It just so happened that when I saw this Wanda, she was the same pretty Black girl from Linden Street in West Oakland. She had moved to the same neighborhood as me! What were the chances?

For some reason, going to church was always required of me. Not Mom, not Dad, just me. I wondered then: Why did only I need church? The only time I didn't go was when we lived a short period of time in East Oakland, and I think that was probably because my parents may not have felt comfortable enough to send me to a predominately white church. From the church at the Lower Bottom to my grandmother's church in Texas to the new church on the corner in Berkeley, they either preached fire and brimstone or underground railroad preaching.

Underground railroad preaching was a combination of preaching and singing a message: *"Bradas and sistas, we goin' to da riva at midnight, mmmm . . . We gonna catch dat train to glory, we gonna see da Lord unto deliverance to freedom, to our heavenly place, amen."* Underground railroad preaching had been used during the time of slavery to signal different parishioners their exit strategy to freedom, and the slave owner and his hired hands would ignore what they thought were the ravings of the slaves. That same system of preaching spilled into many Black churches, but what's funny is that these songs seeped into some Southern white churches as well.

My grandmother's church in Galveston, Texas, was a large and beautiful-looking building. It gave me an understanding and a message that I don't think church is supposed to give you. The preacher would be yelling fire and damnation, and I would start squirming in my seat. Fire and brimstone was the worst for me, because I was a sinner. My grandmother would grab me by the ear, twist it, and tell me: "Be still, boy, and listen to what the Lord is telling you!" I knew I was cooked then, so if I knew it then, I certainly knew it later in life.

I hated going to my grandmother's church because every time I went, I felt that if I were to be hit by a car, run over by a train, hung by white folks, or shot by a Black person, I was going straight to that fire-and-brimstone place called hell that the preacher was yelling about. That was not the answer I had been looking for or the God I wanted to know. It would take me a while—days, even—to get over that message, but in reality it always stayed with me.

When I was in church, Sunday school, or vacation Bible school, I believed there was a God and that all the stories in the Bible were true. However, I never connected them to the point that there could be a personal thing between God and me. I also believed the scary part about going to hell. But I didn't understand how I could be able to prevent going there by my own efforts. Whenever the thought of my spiritual condition would surface, I would cut off that thinking quickly. It was much easier to decide to do questionable things and be accepted by my peers. I had athletic peers, gang-affiliated peers, and pot-smoking peers, but no churchgoing peers. I eventually began to play sports less and started hanging out with friends and smoking pot often.

I would never tell you (or anyone else) that the members

of the churches I attended were not loving people. I knew my grandmother loved me, and I knew my family loved me. However, I never felt a message of love at church—only doom and damnation. I never felt that I was a part of what they were feeling. Whatever that was, I didn't know. I have to admit that I didn't understand much of what was said in those churches other than the damnation part.

■ ■ ■ ■ ■ ■ ■

In my final year of junior high school, I was given the opportunity to become a part of something. I got an invitation to become a member of a gang. You had to be jumped in—in other words, beaten up by the other members. One day, two guys I knew from West Berkeley approached me while I was having a conversation with the gang leader. They informed me that they could get me some alcohol. The gang leader's eyes lit up like a Christmas tree, and he said yes for me.

By this time, we were close to graduating from junior high. One of the girls in our class was giving a big party after our graduation night dance. I let her know how much I was looking forward to her party. She replied, "I heard you were bringing some good stuff."

I smiled like I was a big shot and said, "I sure am, and I will make sure you get some."

The following morning, we had to be present for an assembly at our school. While I was sitting and talking with the gang leader, I heard someone whispering my name to get my attention. Sure enough, it was the two alcohol merchants. I rushed to the back door to meet them, and they had a large shopping bag full of alcohol. Nervously I led them to my locker and put the bag in. As soon as I was closing my locker door, I saw my home-room teacher coming down the hall. She didn't say a word, and I was glad she didn't.

Back at the auditorium, after I had gotten seated again, a counselor and the dean stood right next to my aisle seat. "Mr. Willis, come with us," they said. They escorted me to the dean's office. When I walked into the office, I saw my large shopping bag of alcohol on the dean's desk. My homeroom teacher had told; she knew something suspicious was going on. They called the police, and I was escorted off the campus. Everyone leaving the junior high assembly could see me in handcuffs, on my way to jail.

I used to go to a park called De Fremery Park in **8**
Oakland. One of the streets bordering the park was 18th
Street, and the street at the end of the park was called
Poplar Street. Across the street was a building simply referred
to as 18th and Poplar. This building had much mystery about
it, and it brought a lot of fear to many of us kids for this reason:
it was juvenile jail. One of the scary things about this place is
that there were bullet marks all over the outside of the building.
Apparently, there had been a famous shootout there one night. I
didn't know the details, but it was enough to put fear in all the
young Black kids' hearts. And now, I was about to become one
of their guests.

The police didn't hesitate to take me to this place, but there
was no attempt to get in touch with my parents that I know of,
nor any mention of my parents to me. After I was processed and
dressed in my jail clothes, I was released into the main popula-
tion only to find somebody I knew. It was one of the alcohol
merchants, who had been arrested for stealing pigeons. It seems
that he hadn't wasted any time pursuing another crime.

Everything was concrete and bars. We were let out of our
cells four times a day: breakfast, lunch, dinner, and free time,

which was the most dangerous time of all. During free time, there was always the risk of violence.

It's not wise to turn down a challenge in a place like this. If you do, you're doomed to be bullied for the rest of your stay, and word will follow you on the outside. If I already had darkness within me, I became even darker inside while locked up in this place for kids. Oh, how I wanted to be a kid at home with my parents. But this was where my decisions had gotten me.

After my eventual release to my parents' custody, my mother waited until my dad was not present to ask me about the details of my arrest. We had a meeting with a police officer in Berkeley. After I gave her all the details, she merely said to me, "Eddie, you should have known better."

"Yes, Mama," was all I could say.

Being locked up caused me to act tougher. It was only an act in front of my friends. I thought it was the cool thing to do. I really wasn't tough at all, but I was a survivor. Before I knew it, summer was over, and it was time to go back to school. This time, it was high school. I had some adjustment problems. Oftentimes, I wouldn't go to class. The only class I liked was sociology, which was a totally new frontier to me.

One day in eleventh grade, when I decided not to go to class, one of the counselors caught me walking away from campus, crossing the street. That got me two weeks in a different juvenile detention center. I had to report with my mother to juvenile court at the Berkeley Police Department. That's where I was sentenced to my time at 150th in East Oakland. Here I was again locked up, only this place had no bars. They used thick steel doors with reinforced portal glass in the doors. It was really easy for me to go stir-crazy in a small concrete room. We were let out to have meals, and we were let out for recreation: basketball, cards, dominoes, or just sitting around reading comic books.

Just like at 18th and Poplar, there were no other races in 150th but Black kids, all of whom were looking to make a reputation. One guy showed me how I could smuggle comic books into my room. Unfortunately, anything in rooms was considered contraband. The powers that be decided to have a shakedown of all the rooms. They located my hidden comic books, which put me on restriction, meaning no recreation time. Fortunately, my release date was the following day. I remember one of the officers saying to me, "Oh, you'll be back, Willis. When you do, you will finish your restriction time!"

"No, I'm sorry. You will not be seeing me here again," I replied.

After my time at 150th, I had to report back to court. The judge informed me that rather than returning to Berkeley High, I would be going to McKinley School. McKinley was a reform school for problem kids. Everyone knew that anyone who went to McKinley never got out. To me, this was my social death sentence. People who went to McKinley were looked down upon by everyone else.

The judge told me this: "Mr. Willis, how you respond will determine whether or not you make it back to Berkeley High. If you don't make it through McKinley, you will end up back in front of me, and that will get you another visit to 150th—only this time, for six months. I hope I don't see you again, Mr. Willis."

McKinley School was horrible. Violence was a daily practice. Students smoked on campus. Not a day passed when you didn't hear a student curse out a teacher. The student would be asked to leave the room, but in a day or two, he would return. Business as usual.

The classrooms at McKinley were charmless and inhospitable. They made me wish I had never complained about the classrooms at Berkeley High. Fortunately, there were some classes I enjoyed, like psychology and sociology. I decided to keep my head down and focus on these classes in order to get through alive.

■ ■ ■ ■ ■ ■ ■

One day, I was summoned to my counselor's office and met two professors from UC Berkeley, Professor O'Shea and Professor Koffee. My counselor informed me that these two professors were starting a research project called The McKinley Hood. They believed that in theory, kids' acts of anger and violence masked their psychological wounds that had been inflicted upon them in early childhood. My counselor asked me if I would be interested in going to the psychology department at the university campus two days a week to participate in their research. Professor O'Shea told me that I would get school credit for participating in this project. I was just glad to have the opportunity to get away from McKinley for a couple days out of the week.

The research began with psychoanalysis, then continued with a mentoring phase, and ended with a more academic approach. Over a year and a half, I developed solid relationships with the UC Berkeley staff. A big conference took place at the Hilton Hotel in San Francisco, in which all of us young guys participated in a Q&A session along with the professors. It all turned out to be a success, which enabled Professors O'Shea and Koffee to get even more funding for this program.

One morning at the administration offices, as kids were

running by, I stopped one to find out what was going on. "This is when we find out if we go back to our normal high schools," he said. You could've knocked me over with a feather. I thought I was doing life in this place called McKinley. I had not believed that there was any escape for me. As I approached the crowd, I noticed kids walking past me. Some were fighting back tears. Others wore angry faces. Some were very animated, screaming many profanities.

When I made my way up to one of the officers, he looked up at me and then down at his desk. He began to shuffle through stacks of paperwork. Once he located mine, he looked up with a smile and said, "Mr. Willis, you're on your way back to Berkeley High!" It turned out that I got a bunch of good grades—all As, except for one B, and no trouble. It was nice being back at Berkeley High, especially with a different attitude. As luck would have it, they were offering psychology classes for seniors.

■ ■ ■ ■ ■ ■ ■

Summer was approaching quickly, and my friends and I felt exuberance at this. One night on our way home from visiting friends, my friend Robert and I were stopped by a Berkeley police officer asking us where we were coming from and where we were going. We told him. He got on the radio while we stood by, waiting with bated breath. The policeman let us continue on our way home. For a while we were bummed about the police stopping us, but we soon returned to the excitement of what was about to happen in our lives—including continuing the UC Berkeley program. As we made our way down the street, we were suddenly approached by three fast-oncoming police vehicles that hemmed us in on all sides. One of the police cars had two white women inside. It was an identification pro-cedure—and these two women identified Robert and me as the culprits involved in a robbery. We were taken to jail and charged with grand larceny. It was hard to believe what had happened to us as we sat in that Berkeley jail.

There we were, sitting quietly at a table, overwhelmed with uncertainty and fear of being convicted for something we had not done. Even at our age, it was common knowledge that Black people and other people of color were often put away for things they did not do. We knew that people of all races committed crimes and should be punished for them. However, we also knew that the scales of justice would not often tilt in our favor.

After a night of restless sleep, the morning came. Another day went by before we went to court. Robert and I pleaded not guilty. Some words were spoken by two men at two different tables. We both understood that we were being held over, which ultimately meant more time in jail. Neither one of us was eigh-teen years of age yet, and we did not understand the comings and goings of court procedures. The police, the public defender, and the DA kept questioning us as if our story were going to change, but of course, it couldn't change. Our story never fit the scenario they were trying to place us in: the scenario did not exist.

It was rough spending the week in jail. Neither of us saw our parents. We were worried that our parents didn't have any idea where we were or what was going on. Neither of us knew what the outcome was going to be for our futures. We were in constant fear that our hopes and dreams were in jeopardy.

After that week in jail, we were shipped off to the county prison even though we were just seventeen years old. That was horrifying. I remember the humiliation of being bent over and hit with powdered pesticides. It was hard not to show fear, but I instinctively felt this was not the time to be a whiner. By the time it was all over, I was alone in a six-by-six concrete room with thick-gauged wire mesh for a ceiling. There was a catwalk with a guard that would pace up and down, looking into each cell. I was in the famous Santa Rita County facility that had once been a Japanese internment camp. At the time, I thought, *looks like I've come full circle*. After all, the hospital I had been quarantined in was just like the Santa Rita County Jail. I was trapped, once again. All I could feel was despair.

■ ■ ■ ■ ■ ■ ■

After dinner one night, I felt like the walls were closing in on me. There was nowhere to run and nowhere to hide. What a cruel blow in my life. What was I to expect out of it at this point? Why had I even tried to make it better? When did I ever have the option for something more? The lights went out, but my mind stayed on. So many emotions, so many thoughts, so many tears. I did the best that I could to cry silently into my pillow in the dark. Morning came, and I pondered the reason for my tears the night before. My grief was not only about being locked up in this prison cell. It was the thought of having been so close to doing something I would've enjoyed in life through psychology and sociology. I would have had fun! I would have gotten paid! And it was all wiped away by this power structure that considered me a threat to their way of life, when I didn't even know what life was really about. I had so many questions, and there were no answers in sight. These were tears of injustice, tears of pain, and tears of discrimination. Something else, however, took the place of those tears, and its name was rage.

After a few days in the Santa Rita County Jail, I signed up for going to church Sunday. I figured I could get out of my cell for a while. Three days later, church time arrived, and I couldn't have been happier to go to church and see my friend Robert. Before things started, we had the opportunity to talk a little bit about our situation. We didn't have a clue how we were going to get out of this mess. Two white women said that we had committed this crime. It was their word against ours, and we knew we didn't stand a chance.

During the church service, I listened to the chaplain's message of forgiveness. Much of it, however, was blocked out by my internal prayers to get out of this predicament.

Monday was court day. After rising at four o'clock in the morning, we took a long trip all the way back to the Berkeley court, where we were placed in what was called a bull pen. A bull pen was for animals—but I wasn't an animal.

A judgment was finally made to release us to our parents, so we had to go back to Santa Rita to be processed out. Except there was one problem—my parents weren't there. I asked one of the arresting officers why they hadn't tried to reach my parents. The officer told me then that they had indeed spoken to my father. Upon finding out I was in jail, my father could only reply, "Just keep him." My own father believed me to be guilty of the crime that we had been arrested for. Had he not seen the change in me? Or was it too late for him to believe that I could change?

Fortunately, the sheriff's department allowed me to be released to Robert's parents' custody, so I stayed with their family. They treated me like a son. My mother, however, had no idea what was going on with me, because she had heard that I was staying somewhere else and was trying to give me my independence. I ran into her one evening and she was so glad to see me, but deep down inside, I kind of blamed her for allowing Daddy to do what he did. She wanted to know why I had decided not to stay at home, and I told her what had happened. It turned out she knew nothing about the situation. She told me that as long as she had breath, and as long as I was doing the right thing, I had a home to come back to. With that we hugged, and I again felt what a loving family could be.

■ ■ ■ ■ ■ ■ ■

We still had a court hearing concerning the charges against us. When that day arrived, the plaintiff's story contained too many inaccuracies. The judge had heard enough and threw the case out of court. That disaster was behind us. Whoever committed this so-called crime—if there was a crime—that's something I'll never know.

After the relief of the dismissed court case set in, we were all very excited. Robert and I would be allowed to participate in the Berkeley summer program again, which meant we would receive $380 per month over the summer. It made us feel like we actually had a chance to go to college. There was hope for the future again.

All good things must come to an end, however. In our case, the state pulled the plug on the funding of projects like these for the state budget's sake. Ours was one of many projects that was ended by budget cuts. The kids involved were just beginning to respond positively to the program. For us to learn that we were no longer going to be a part of each other's lives caused a lot of anger and pain. We were finished, and everybody sadly said their goodbyes. Professor O'Shea helped me get a job for minimum wage in the political science department for the rest of the summer. However, he didn't—and couldn't—quell the anger and rage I felt toward the system and the elusive, so-called American Dream. I began to slip into the darkness of my thoughts, and my actions soon followed.

■ ■ ■ ■ ■ ■ ■

Again living at home as school was ending, I became more of a problem to my dad. We'd get into verbal confrontations, and my responses to him were borderline disrespectful. Although Daddy would never put his hands on me, he threatened that when I turned eighteen years old, I needed to have someplace else to be, because in his words, "We can't have two men in the house at the same time." None of my friends in my neighborhood seemed to be getting pressured to move out, so why *me*? Again I questioned the relationship and role of a father.

Well, the time had come. I was seventeen years old, about to turn eighteen, and I couldn't seem to find a job. After so many days of disappointment due to my fruitless job search, I decided to go visit my friend Willie. One of his sisters let me into the house and I went to the bedroom, where Willie and Robert were.

I saw Willie and Robert with a large spoon along with some liquid and a syringe. They immediately said, "Eddie, you've got to try this!" After much persuasion and coaxing from my friends, I finally conceded. Suddenly, it seemed like the whole world lit up. There was a rushing sensation in my mind. It gave me an elation I'd never felt. I wondered if I was going to survive it. Robert and Willie were looking at me with great joy on their faces, as I was now feeling what they were feeling.

"Where in the world did you get this? What is it?" I asked. They told me that it was crank—in other words, methamphetamine. This was my introduction to intravenous drugs. I had gone from feeling low and worthless to feeling like I was at the top of the mountain. Like Superman, I felt that there was nothing I couldn't do. And I liked that feeling. That was what hooked me and all of the rest of us as well.

This drug swept through the Bay Area like a wildfire. Soon it was embedded deeply in the entire region. Sometimes I would wonder if there was someone who thought, *let's use the Bay Area to try this drug out*. After all, marijuana had been successful, LSD had been successful, mescaline had been successful, and now crank was another success. Then heroin was the next drug craze. We had all known that all of these drugs existed, but suddenly they became readily available. There was a deluge of drugs not only in the Bay Area, but in California at large.

Berkeley seemed liberal, but I was beginning **10**
to wonder why no one would hire me. Everyone
I had to face was white. Could that have been the
reason? After making constant trips to the employment office,
I realized that there were some employees that worked there
who were Black. They seemed like the "Uncle Tom" type, or a
"house slave" type. That term referred to the African Americans
who had lighter skin. Back in slavery times, the lighter-skinned
slaves were the ones who worked in the household, as opposed
to the darker-skinned slaves who worked in the field.

Regardless of what I thought about them, they were doing
something I wasn't—working. I was beginning to get desperate.
I was doing more speed and less looking for work. One of the
biggest crank dealers in the region happened to be an old friend
of mine. Many who knew him wanted to use his services but
were afraid. So, they ordered through me. I charged them taxes
for both money and drugs. This job allowed me to support my
own drug habit. Another friend of mine who was a big-time
crank merchant was a real gangster, with guys around him that
carried guns. With me, there was no fear from others. Many
would come to me so that I could purchase for them. Thieves

who were willing to trade their valuables for drugs would also visit me sometimes. That's how I would get nice pieces of clothing or jewelry.

I spent a lot of time hanging around the hippie crowd. The rock-and-rollers. The free lovers. All around the university and up and down Telegraph Avenue was a hippie lifestyle where women were free, drugs were free, alcohol was free, and living was free. So, I crashed at a lot of places. The majority of hippies I knew were white, and many of them came from affluent families. Seemingly, their parents let their kids do whatever they wanted. Some of their parents even joined in on the free love lifestyle and devil-may-care attitude.

■ ■ ■ ■ ■ ■ ■

Back in that day, we were all willing vessels. Like sheep to the slaughter, we would submit ourselves to the government. We would receive letters after we reached the age of eighteen directing us to report to our local draft board to be processed for military service. A group of five of us went down and went through the process, but only three of us were accepted. Robert and I didn't make the cut. Robert didn't make it because they said he had flat feet. I didn't make it because of a problem they said I had with my albumin. I had no idea what that was. I had to go through a series of tests at a local clinic in Berkeley for eight weeks. I know now that the cause of this albumin was my drug use.

Drugs were a constant part of my life then. This came at a price, of course. I had a lot of stressors in my life. Pressure I was getting from my dad about finding a place to stay. Not being able to find a job.

This was a very lonely and dark time in my life. I didn't know what was to become of me. I still said the Lord's Prayer every night, but I was beginning to feel that I had to stop. In my mind, I had no right to pray because of what I had become: a bum. That's what I felt like I was. I wasn't able to take care of myself. I wasn't a responsible person like my dad who went to work every day and took care of his family. What family could I have had in my situation? None! We would starve, because no one would give me a job! Fortunately, I had heard of a place called the Urban League, where one could be helped with finding employment. I went there and filled out a bunch of papers. They gave me extensive interviews to see if they could help get me a job. After leaving, I felt like even though I didn't walk away with a job, I had accomplished something.

I had plenty of time to think about my plight in life. I was a young Black man in America that couldn't find a job, and all I did each and every day was use dope and hang out with people who didn't seem to have the same problems that I had. As far as I could tell, the system would not allow someone like me access to the American Dream.

One day as I walked toward my apartment, I **11** saw an old buddy, Wayne, going up to my door with a gorgeous Black woman wearing a black turtleneck sweater, tight black jeans, and some knee-high patent-leather black boots. I remember wondering, *what in the world is he doing with her? And why are they going to my apartment?* I had known Wayne ever since the seventh grade, but I had no idea that he was coming to see me. Wayne had just been in the army. He had been stationed over in Germany. Wayne turned and saw me.

"Ed! I was just looking for you! What's going on, man? How are you doing?"

Wayne had told the young lady who was with him that he knew a guy who could get some high-quality marijuana. Wayne was right. I *did* have the ability and the connections to get it. I went with Wayne and the young woman in Wayne's new GTO. We headed up to Telegraph Avenue, near the UC Berkeley campus. I approached one guy and named the strain I wanted. He gave it to me, I gave him the money, and that was all. When I got back to the car with Wayne and the young lady, they were excited and amazed—especially the young lady. By this point, I had realized that this woman happened to be somebody I had known since the fourth grade. I may have mentioned her before. I played pogo stick with her when I lived in West Oakland. I knew her when I was in junior high school. I hadn't recognized her at first. It was Wanda! She was all grown up. I wasn't sure if she recognized me. I almost hoped that she didn't, because I didn't think I had grown up as nicely as she had.

Wayne drove us to Wanda's house. Upon entering, we were greeted by Wanda's sister, who was very jovial. We smoked, listened to music, and danced. We had a wonderful time. Wanda seemed to be interested in me. I couldn't take my eyes off of her, either. It had gotten to be about 2:00 a.m., and Wayne was about to go home. He wanted to give me a ride home, but Wanda wouldn't have it. She insisted that I stay, and I did. Wanda was amazing. Not only was she beautiful, but she was kind. Full of fun. She never seemed to put any pressure on me at all. All she cared about was that she and I got along and had fun together. This was a new experience for me. Never had I ever felt this kind of closeness to a woman, though I'd had plenty of experience with the opposite sex. Still—there was a lot for me to learn about relationships, and I was beginning to learn with Wanda.

∎ ∎ ∎ ∎ ∎ ∎ ∎

The honeymoon stage of our relationship soon began to fade. It wasn't because we were having conflict with one another, but because I knew sooner or later, I was going to have to pay my way. I didn't have a problem with that—that's just the way life is. I was still struggling with finding employment. At this stage of my life, though, I was willing to do just about anything. The opportunity came for me to dig holes around telephone poles with a pick and shovel. I would come back to

Wanda with swollen, blistered, painful hands. I needed to prove to her that I would work—no matter what. Wanda, however, insisted that I stop doing manual labor, so I stopped and looked for something else. I began to finally have a sense of belonging. Wanda made me feel at home all the time, but she had higher aspirations than mine. She was looking for an even better place to stay. She lived in a really nice Victorian house, but she was searching for more.

One morning, the strangest thing happened. To this day, I still can't explain it. I woke up one day to find a pound of marijuana on the dresser. I asked several friends who had been by our house for various gatherings, but none of them would admit that they were responsible for leaving it. So, I used it as a means of gathering finances—in other words, I began to sell marijuana.

Sometimes, I would be out and about with marijuana for both my personal use and for sale. As I went through the day trying to make money, I would often run into people who were trying to get me to join the Black Panther Party. I didn't know much about it, but I would see people gathering for rallies at Provo Park in Berkeley. On the other side of the avenue from the park was the Berkeley Police Department. Civil rights rallies and Black Panther rallies were taking place all around me. Familiar faces would always come up to me and ask me about the marijuana I had. In the process, many would also inquire why I wouldn't join their cause. I replied then that I didn't know enough about it to become a member. But things would change.

The protest against the Vietnam War was growing larger and larger. Members of the Black Panther Party spoke against it. Malcolm X was against it. Martin Luther King was against it. Many were speaking out against this war in Indochina. I became more enraged at the idea of Black men going to fight wars for a country that didn't care one bit about them. During this time of transformation in America, Americans of African descent were becoming more educated about all of the contributions we had made throughout the entire world. We realized that we should no longer hang our heads down as if we were second-class citizens. We as a people deserved the same opportunities and rights as all other people! It was time to educate ourselves about the facts. It was time to understand that we came from a culture of dignity. Black people were no longer going to carry the physical, mental, and emotional burdens placed on our backs. We demanded rights and privileges according to the Constitution of the United States that were meant for all men. The Constitution acted as the foundation on which Huey P. Newton made his stand and founded the Black Panther Party.

It was pretty good business selling weed around civil rights rallies. I often cruised those areas selling my wares. I was down at Provo Park when three familiar young Black women tried to recruit me into the Black Panther Party. They were beckoning for me to join them, so I stood with them for a while. As I listened to the rhetoric of the speakers, I became angrier and angrier at the plight of my people. I began to understand that we had been led astray. America had not been honest with us economically, politically, or socially. I would often go back home and share what I had heard at these rallies with Wanda. We both had serious concerns about the way this country was going and realized that things were going to end up with so many people angry. I originally thought we'd wait and see how things turn out, but over time I found myself wanting to do more.

In those days, I'd often come up short financially. This was an issue that got to be a burden. This also caused me to make destructive decisions. I remember making one decision so that Wanda and I could pay the rent and buy our groceries. I grabbed a .22 automatic gun and asked a friend to come along for backup. I had everything planned out—exactly what I would say, and exactly what I was willing to do to accomplish my mission and collect on payments due. I was going to say to the cashier, "Do you want to die for the white man's money? If not, then give me mine!" This is exactly what I said.

With money in hand, we heard shots firing behind us. I turned around and immediately started returning his fire as my friend and I split. I remember the odd sensation of feeling the heat and bullets whizzing by my face and body. I returned fire, and my friend ducked behind a building. I fell behind the fence unharmed and without fear. I heard police sirens as I cut through the center of San Pablo Park. I saw police cars racing down toward San Pablo Avenue. I had to be very careful about making my way home. I had to make sure not to seem like I was running away from something.

I finally arrived back to Wanda, who had been worried sick about me. I asked if the friend who was watching my back had arrived. Wanda said no, he had not. I began to tell her everything that had happened. The more I told her, the more fearful she became at the thought of just one of those bullets entering my body.

Was it all worth it?

"All I know is that we can pay the rent and get groceries," Wanda said. But I could tell she was still upset.

········

The "liberal" dream of Berkeley was a fraud. While the Southern whites would talk down to you, the Berkeley whites played it cool with you. They didn't hate "the Negro"; they loved you—or rather, they loved the symbolism you represented. They might not know—or care to know—your name. I made them look urbane, hip, and aware. However, being the token Black friend doesn't pay well. But I was not naïve. A young no-goodnik, unable (and unwilling) to Uncle Tom my way into some menial job? Maybe. Unemployed? Basically. High? Usually! I *was* the stereotype that white people had constructed about us—the stereotype used to ensure that the wealth and influence stayed in the hands with a little less melanin. I was what white Americans feared.

Some folks don't realize that the drug trade and the civil rights movement occurred at the same time—often within shouting distance of each other. Some civil rights protestors were clean, but not everyone. They used along with the rest of us. Two scenes taking place on the same stage in the same theater. Sometimes, I used civil rights protests for business. A lot of people in the same place, looking not only to march for freedom, but also to get a buzz (for a moment or two). Say what you will about civil rights, but I was no ideologue. I was a businessman, and I looked for markets. While Wanda never said anything to me about the rallies and the movement, I always felt her shadow. Her presence compelled me to refine myself—to consider myself with a higher stature.

As I roamed around the rallies looking for clients, friends approached me. *Ed, you ever think about becoming a Panther?* I wasn't *really* that sort. That was for the die-hards. I preferred to live day to day, working this job or that. All this Panther business seemed to be for people more serious than I was. But no one could ignore that Black bodies came home by the day from that war in Vietnam. I might have been a bum, but I was a bum who understood who cared about him, and who didn't. East Oakland didn't care. California didn't care. And certainly the United States didn't care. Even the most liberal of the liberals cared more about "the Negro" than they did about individual Black folks.

My first rallies had been business opportunities. But soon, I began to listen. Conversion is a funny experience. Our motives begin to change. Some people become Jews, Latter-day Saints, Catholics, or Muslims for social advantages or for access to networks. I originally attended civil rights rallies to help people get high. But in time, I realized that what those men in suits and berets were saying resonated with my experience. Everything I had seen—the storefront church, Black folks killing each other, Black folks getting high, Black folks working their tails off— made sense. It wasn't just me. I wasn't just a bum. My friends weren't just bums. We had been duped and led astray from what this country was about. The promise of success, access, and happiness was sewn into everything we had heard about what this country is meant to represent, but we were kept from having any part of it.

And yet, for three hundred years, Black folks had carried the burden of making America run—and for no reward. Slaves, servants, now war soldiers. For a little pay and a home, we Black folks were willing to take up a gun and shoot when we were told. And I had been complicit. At one time, I had been willing to do that myself.

I had always thought that the Constitution was a pretty good document. It kept the government in check (it said). It claimed that although there were some things that America could not do, Eddie Willis is guaranteed *something*. America gives freely. But, America also takes—and demands—a sacrifice. Water and oil, jobs and mortgages. If Black lives had to pay the price for America's prosperity, so let it be done and decreed.

I decided to take up arms. Folks didn't have the time to think about how they would earn their next breath. We knew it in our bones, in our gut, that we had a right to life and liberty. No one needed to say it. John Wayne walked around with his gun proudly—and he valued what was his, not waiting for some pretentious fellow in a bow tie to hand him his rights.

My entry into the Panther Party was unremarkable. I smoked and thought, thought and smoked. And one day, I realized that I had had a bum deal. I realized that my life wasn't much on its own—I needed to be part of something great. White folks looking on would have been scared out of their minds: they just saw Black inner-city folks milling around talking to each other. And a lot of us. That scares white folks. I get it, but they must know that the world made for us scared us even more.

The media told white Americans that the Panthers hated America. That was not so. The feeling of patriotism loomed large in the hearts of many of these Black Americans in spite of how they had been treated. We had a right to fight for the country we dreamed of, too. I loved the vibe of the party. They had a well-thought-out plan of where they were going, what they wanted, and how they would get there. I had to decide if I would be willing to give up my life for those principles. I went to the party headquarters. I visited with David Hilliard, the captain of the party, who then introduced me to George Murphy, the minister of education. I was no longer just Ed, the unemployed statistic of a Black man wandering the streets. I was Ed the Black Panther. Ed the Revolutionary. At age twenty when I looked at myself in the mirror, I finally saw John Wayne. I attended these rallies wandering around in a haze. It was like going to that storefront church—only this time, it mattered. This might not have been the Holy Spirit, but it was the spirit of the race. The spirit of the Cause. I was a part of something, and I had a purpose. I was a Black Panther—and like a panther, I would not attack until pushed into a corner.

But what did Black Panthers *do*? We could talk of the Cause, of rights, of freedom—but Panthers also had tasks. We needed money. We were making a Black nation—and nations don't run for free! But we didn't have the Rockefellers or the Rothschilds coughing up money to get us off the ground. So we declared war. Being a Black Panther wasn't about complaining, griping, begging, or borrowing. It was about believing, just as my mother had taught me, that I could help myself. We declared war using the American language of weaponry and firearms. And, if Blacks had to die for victory, then their deaths would not be in vain.

The Black Panthers were political—let no one tell you that we were just a bunch of random hoodlums. We believed in ten platforms:

1. We wanted freedom—power to determine the destiny of our Black community. We would not be free until we could do so.

2. We wanted full employment—the federal government

had the responsibility to provide opportunity for every man to have employment and an income. If businesses did not comply, their businesses should be stripped from business owners and placed in the hands of the community.

3. We wanted an end to the capitalist exploitation of the Black community. Just as the Germans had killed six million Jews, so had American racism led to the death of millions of Black people during the transatlantic slave trade, Jim Crow persecution, and throughout the whole of American history. Given the cost inflicted on our people, it was only right that Black people be given their "forty acres and a mule" promised to them at the end of the Civil War.

4. We wanted decent housing. If landlords would not comply, the federal government should commandeer housing and make it into cooperatives so that Black people, with government support, could build their own housing.

5. We wanted education that exposed the true nature of this American society—education that would give to our people a knowledge of self.

6. We held that Black men should be exempt from military service. We would not fight for a government that did not protect us. We would certainly not kill other people of color who, like us, were victims of the white government.

7. We wanted an end—immediate and complete—to police brutality in our Black communities. We could put a stop to it in the same way white men had done for years: arm ourselves.

8. We wanted Black men in jail to be released, as they had not received fair trials.

9. We wanted Black people to be tried by Black people,

as the Constitution holds that they should be given a jury trial by their peers.

10. We wanted land, bread, housing, education, clothing, justice, and peace. To help accomplish that, we started programs providing free breakfast for children, distributed clothing to those in need, sponsored schools, offered legal aid and transportation assistance, and more.

After surveying the ten platforms of the Black Panther Party, one might believe that these demands were unreasonable. One might think that these demands were even bizarre. I can understand how that might be—many have not had challenges with buying a home, receiving medical assistance, or having the best education because of the color of their skin.

■ ■ ■ ■ ■ ■ ■

As for Wanda and me, our introductions to the party started off differently. A friend invited Wanda to go with her to a Panther rally at Tech High School. There, Wanda heard the tenets of pride, dignity, and self-awareness directly from Huey P. Newton, the minister of defense and cofounder of the Black Panther Party. His words had a powerful effect on her: she felt the need to be a part of something that big and important. Even though our introductions to the party were different, the outcome was the same. Wanda was more interested in the nurturing part, however—helping rising generations of Black children to get the resources and support they needed to succeed. I was more interested in the self-defense part.

The Black Panthers started the breakfast program for children in this country long before that type of assistance was widely available. Wanda was a big part of that program. Local

stores would donate
food of all kinds to the
Black Panther Party,
who would not only
distribute the food, but
prepare it. The women
of the party would pre-
pare breakfast before
school for the children
to start the day off with
healthy nutrition. Other
services that the Black
Panther Party would
provide for all commu-
nities included legal aid
and medical assistance.

The Free Breakfast for Children Program,
run by the Black Panther Party, 1970

The most full-service clinic was in West Oakland. People were
able to receive help with housing and even senior citizens' services. There were nearly sixty different community services that
the Black Panther Party would provide. One of the most effective and necessary services was their street surveillance against
police occupation and brutality. The Black Panthers would get
plenty of political pushback from those in power. Police departments all over knew that one of the party's slogans was "power
[lies] in the barrel of a gun."

It was no secret that we had our share of guns. In addressing
the police patrolling and surveillance issue, we would usually set
ourselves up in pairs of two brothers or sisters that would keep
watch if someone was having difficulty with "police occupiers"
(as I referred to them). It was a very effective method. Most of
the time, police officers would show a little more restraint when

they had a couple of witnesses looking on and keeping notes. Many of us witnesses would write down badge and vehicle numbers and record the circumstances by which the citizen was being detained or harassed.

There were times when things didn't turn out the way we wanted. Many Panthers also ended up being arrested. Some police officers could not or would not restrain themselves. They would become even more agitated and aggressive. Citizens were making a stand because officers were not accountable for how they policed the community. More often than not, though, both the citizen and the Black Panther Party member would be released with no charge within a few hours. Often, the police would use petty excuses like a ticket warrant that would give them the cause to continue their harassment, sometimes with no charge at all. Needless to say, this made a lot of Black people proud to have a militant policing group like the Black Panther Party watching over them to make sure that they were safe. Black people have never felt safe in their communities. Only with the emergence of the Black Panthers had they begun to believe that it was possible.

■ ■ ■ ■ ■ ■ ■

I remember being apprehensive about telling my parents that I had become a member of the Black Panthers. Walking up the steps, I anticipated that I would get a negative reaction. To my surprise, there was a brief smile from my dad. "You just be careful," my mother admonished. I told her I would. "It was only a matter of time until you young people were going to get tired of putting up with the things that we, and many before us, put up with for years," my mother said. My father asked me if

I carried a gun. I told him no, which was true—I didn't carry a gun because I didn't own one at the time. In fact, I didn't even know if the Panthers distributed them to us. I would later find out that they did not. I had to figure out the weapons thing on my own.

I did get the opportunity to go out a couple of times with the Black Panther Party to shooting ranges. My profits from selling marijuana soon gave me the capital I needed to buy whatever firearms I wanted. But of course, I had to buy them from the street. I decided that stockpiling firearms would be the safest route. Not all Panthers had their own guns, but I was a soldier—that's all I wanted to be, and that's all I was. I wasn't trying to go up the ranks or gain any privileges—if there were any to be had.

Being a Black Panther was a thing of pride, yet the party didn't seem to have a screening process for their members. There were a lot of brothers from the hood that joined the Black Panthers because they had axes to grind against the white man or someone else. Regardless, they would use the Black Panther mantle as a reason to fulfill their desires of revenge or assault. There were also Black nationalist groups. The Black Muslim organization that once had the honorable Malcolm X as a member believed that all whites were bad and were against all who were Black. The Black Panther Party did not subscribe to this ideology, because they often had affiliates of European origin. The politicians and the media would have the masses thinking the Black Panthers were automatically against all whites, however. We were up against those in power even in trying to show that we were not an enemy.

I would never claim that my experience in the
party was the same as that of other members. I only
know that I have my own experience, which took **14**
an interesting turn after a while. One day, Wanda came to me
and explained that there were Black Panthers who were treat-
ing the young girls inappropriately. In other words, sexual harassment was occurring. Wanda expressed great disdain for this
behavior, as it was hypocritical. One of the things the Black
Panthers spoke against was sexual exploitation.

James Brown had come out with a song called "Say It
Loud—I'm Black and I'm Proud," and Black people had begun
to believe it. Black Panthers would often refer to the pride of
Black people. They would refer to the contributions that Black
people had made to the world's societies, only to be made to feel
less than. So the language changed concerning Black women especially. Black women were no longer just women—they were
queens. Much of the new nomenclature brought on somewhat
better behavior. The treatment of women was still lacking, but it
was much better than it had been before.

This inappropriate behavior within the party was unacceptable to Wanda, and it was unacceptable to me—but not to

the point where I would quit the party. Wanda and other sisters would try to counsel the younger women on what it meant to be a responsible woman and Panther. But Wanda could see the destruction these men had wrought upon the women of the party. In her eyes, much of the progress of the Panthers had unraveled because of it. It was too much for her to bear, so she quit.

Wanda had found a new place for us to move. It was in a better neighborhood. We moved two houses off the corner of Shattuck Avenue and Emerson Street. Our house was also around the corner from the new Black Panther headquarters. The old headquarters on Grove Street about half a mile from our old place had been shot up by the Oakland Police Department. After moving, we had exhausted all of our funds and were in need of supplies. This too was one of the reasons I had joined the Black Panther Party—it meant being part of a community that would help you out when you were in need, and that was something I had always desired.

I remember the nightmare that may have changed my life a little. I dreamt that I walked out of the house down the stairs to the driveway. Down the sidewalk, a very, very large white man with a white shirt, suspenders, and black pants walked by me. I got behind him with the thought of robbing him for his wallet so I could provide for myself, Wanda, and her little daughter Traci, who I had become a father to. My desire to get what I needed was great, and I did not care about his size. I only cared about fulfilling the needs that my small family had. I saw a stick while walking. I grabbed it to hit the man with it—and suddenly awoke in a cold sweat. I realized that I'd had a nightmare.

The next day passed without any of my job leads coming through. That night, I decided to go for a walk and think. As I walked down my driveway, lo and behold, a very large white man in a white shirt with suspenders and black pants walked past me, just like in the nightmare I'd had the previous night. As I followed behind him, I could not believe that I was reliving my dream. Was this an offering? An opportunity that I should take advantage of? As we walked, I saw a stick. Right then, I decided I would not attack this man. I would not inflict pain on this man who knew nothing of my own pain. Being discriminated against didn't give me license to be a crook, a robber, a thief, or even a murderer. I had no way of knowing what the outcome of this would be. I had no way of knowing if I would even survive the attack. With these realizations in mind, I stopped walking, turned around, and headed back home.

■ ■ ■ ■ ■ ■ ■

We had an electric coil heater. I plugged it in, got a few pieces of bread, spread margarine on the bread, and put the slices in front of the heater. We ate toast for dinner that night. The next morning, I decided to give my mother a call so that she knew that I was all right. Around the corner from us was a phone booth by the service station. My mother was really glad to hear from me. She had some news.

"Eddie, the FBI have been here looking for you, and this place called Cal Book Company called you for a job," she told me. With that, I was totally excited—so excited that I didn't care about the FBI part. Just before I hung up the phone, I saw a plain car with two white men dressed in suits inside coming down the street. I knew they had to be from the FBI. As they passed by me in the phone booth, I chatted with my mother longer to figure out if my suspicions were true. What was I to do? I couldn't think of any reason why they would present any threat to Wanda and her daughter Traci. I did know that my friend George was AWOL and staying in our house. George was one of the boys I had gone to the draft board with to enlist in the military. He had only arrived at our house the night before.

I came out of the phone booth and headed down the street. As I approached our new home, I could see over our backyard fence. The two agents were standing on the sidewalk. One was writing on his notepad while the other one was questioning our next-door neighbor, an elderly Black woman. As she talked, the other one wrote. She looked in my direction, saw me, and gave me a nod as if to warn me. I made my way around the block and hid behind some bushes by a neighbor's house. I waited until the agents drove away and then I proceeded home. I found out from Wanda that the agents were there questioning her about George's whereabouts. While the agents were questioning Wanda, little Traci had been running up and down the hall yelling, "Uncle George, Uncle George, Uncle George!" Wanda was trying to make her settle down and be quiet. The agents didn't have a clue at all, but if they had looked just down the hall toward our living room, they would've seen George's feet hanging off the end of our couch in the doorway.

I was not off the hook with the FBI. Despite
initially being dismissed from service, there was now
a little thing called draft evasion that I was dealing with, because I had decided that I was not going to go to
Vietnam even if I became eligible. My mother and Wanda knew
that I had kept two appointments with an agent who called
himself Agent Smith near downtown Berkeley. This agent inquired about me not showing up for my tour of duty. I explained to him that I did not feel the need to be a part of the
military campaign against the Vietnamese. He warned me that if
I did not report on the next date that was given to me, I would
be apprehended and charged as a draft dodger. He also made
some light inquiries concerning my affiliation with the Black
Panther Party. I informed him that I had the same belief system
as they did. I also informed him that if he *really* needed to know
anything about the Black Panther Party, all he needed to do was
report to the headquarters on Shattuck Avenue and present his
inquiries there at the counter. With that, I left.

My friend Robert knew that the FBI had been asking
about me. So, Robert went and did something I never would've
thought of. One night, there was a knock on the door while

I was sitting in the living room listening to some jazz. I saw Wanda cross the hall and open the front door. I couldn't see who she greeted, but their tone was pleasant. She entered back into the hallway and looked down the hall at me. "You'll never guess who's here," she said. The first one up the stairs was Robert, and right behind him was Professor O'Shea with a six-pack of beer in hand! Professor O'Shea shared with me that Robert had informed him of my difficulties with the FBI. After a couple of beers and my detailed story about the draft board and Agent Smith, the professor made a request.

"Eddie, would you write a small autobiography of your childhood for me?" he asked.

"What?" I asked.

"Just trust me—please do it, and bring it back to my office when it's done."

"I will, but I don't know how this will help me," I said.

"But I do," he remarked.

I began my autobiography that night. It included all of the abuses that I had experienced. I had witnessed murder at the age of six. I'd had different clashes with bullies, police, and more. I wrote down everything. Two days later, I took what I had written to Professor O'Shea's office. I sat quietly as he read. He told me that he would be at my house that evening to give me some paperwork. That night, he showed up with paperwork in hand. There was a one-page letter with instructions from him stating that I was not supposed to let just anyone have this paperwork as I went through the induction center once again. The thought of that did alarm me, because I had no intentions of going to Vietnam. He assured me that if I did as he instructed, and gave the letter to the last officer of the day, all would be well. So I did as he said.

I reported to the induction center on the date that I had been instructed to by the government. I went through all the tests and took all the exams. Toward the end of the day, I came to a Black sergeant who had a lab coat on and was sitting at a desk. He was curious about the letter that I had in my hand. He asked if he could see it, and I told him no—the letter was for the last person I was to see, which was the person after him. He assured me that he would not harm the letter or keep it, but that he only wanted to read it. After he read the letter, he looked at me with disgust and hatred. The end of my letter stated that because of the traumatic experiences in my life, I was more likely to turn and kill my commanding officer than to kill a Vietcong soldier.

"You are a disgrace to your country, and a disgrace to your race," he said. I thought it would be better for me to not reply because I was in enemy territory. I moved on to the last person. He was in uniform and a lab coat, but he had two bars on his collar. He read my letter, and without hesitation, took a stamp and stamped my paperwork. The stamp read 1Y, which meant that only in national emergencies would this person be called to serve. Needless to say, when I read that, I could not contain myself. I felt a huge weight lifted off of not just my body, but my soul as well. My whole life seemed to have been restored. I couldn't wait to get home to tell Wanda the good news. Once again, Professor O'Shea had come to my rescue.

■ ■ ■ ■ ■ ■ ■

I took a job in a bookstore, continued selling marijuana, and began to buy weapons on the black market. Wanda and I made and stored some Molotov cocktails and kept them in cold storage until we needed them. One evening, I was assigned by the party to be security at a rally at my old high school, Berkeley High. That night, the Peace and Freedom Party leader Jerry Rubin was speaking onstage with a joint of marijuana and a jug of wine in hand. He smoked and drank as he spoke. Eldridge Cleaver from the Black Panthers was the next speaker, and I was posted onstage behind him. When Cleaver took the stage, Rubin handed him the joint and the jug and hugged him. Cleaver accepted them all. I cringed, because I felt that they were sending a negative message. It wasn't about the hug; it was about the rest of it. I didn't want the message of the Black Panthers to get tied up with being all about drugs and partying.

I served in security detail: protect the man at the top from roughnecks looking to cause problems. I hadn't been a gun handler before, but it felt good to be one. The world looked at us and saw an army of armed Black men. We sold ourselves as revolutionaries. Boy, did Eldridge Cleaver know how to scare white people. If someone left the room while he was speaking, he unleashed upon them a litany of insults and swearing. He made it clear to all in attendance that you do not leave while Eldridge Cleaver speaks. I didn't like that. I didn't believe that's what the Panthers were about. *What if he was just going to the restroom?* I thought. At another rally in De Fremery Park, Cleaver seemed to use the foulest language he could possibly come up with.

Don't misunderstand me: I had a mouth too, but only in private. I knew that not all or even most Black folks appreciated that kind of talk—especially the churchgoing kind that were present at this rally. One must be able to read the room. The attendants of Black Panther rallies weren't the ghetto rats that many white people might have imagined them being. But with that kind of talk, I felt that they might think we aimed to be disrespectful to others. We weren't just speaking to the Blacks from the ghetto. We were speaking to Black lawyers, Black doctors, Black accountants, Black dentists, and Black churchgoers too. I believed that Cleaver cared more about his own image than about his language.

There were many Black people who didn't quite know what to think about the Panthers at this point. Many didn't know if they were troublemakers or not. Some felt that the Black Panthers' actions were setting Black people back from all the progress that had been made. Cleaver had bragged in private about raping women, robbing, stealing, and looting. To him, he was raging against the machine. To me, he was showboating about horrific acts. Why would anyone brag about harming someone? He swore like a sailor, but admittedly, his knowledge ran deep. There was a reason he was our minister of information. He could expound on the depth and breadth of America's structural racism.

Being a Black Panther was not supposed to be an act of raw, unbridled anger, but an act of self-dignity. I didn't hate myself anymore. I didn't hate West Oakland or East Oakland. We Blacks had been alienated from one another. Cleaver's words cut through the apathy. Peppered with obscenities, he was the one who could speak truth in a way that made us want to call him Professor Cleaver. We were not bandits. We were community activists committed to self-defense, free speech, and neighborhood development.

The police did not see us as an activist group. **16** They considered us to be terrorists. We, however, saw the police as our oppressors. Sure, they wanted to protect people—white people. They wanted to protect order—their order. The police wanted to enjoy full reign of fire because we said and did things that made many white people feel uncomfortable. In 1967, our founder, Huey P. Newton, allegedly shot a policeman named John Frey during a heated exchange in a traffic stop. When he was locked up, the party told the world that the sky was the limit. That meant we would launch a guerrilla war against the Oakland police oppressors if Newton was not released—at least, that's how I interpreted it. Many of the members were discussing it among themselves. Regardless, we had seen too much.

Only a few days after Dr. Martin Luther King was killed in Tennessee in April 1968, the Oakland police killed Bobby Hutton, a teenage boy devoted to the party. Eldridge Cleaver and some other party members—some of whom I knew personally—had been transporting guns when the Oakland police ambushed them. Young Bobby Hutton came running out of the building, allegedly surrendering with his hands up. Quick

to the trigger, the Oakland police shot him. Hutton's death gar-
nered all kinds of media attention. Even Marlon Brando came
to his funeral.

■ ■ ■ ■ ■ ■ ■

Every time the police attacked us, we were going to defend
ourselves, but the police were not in a negotiating posture this
time. We always had to be on the lookout, so we planned our
moves as a military operation. I was told to report and serve
as a detail at a San Francisco State College rally. Bobby Seale,
Black Panther cofounder, hit his talk out of the park. Coming
off the high of another rally, talking big things and big dreams,
we crawled back into our vehicles to head back to Oakland.
We were a five-car caravan. Three of the cars kept going toward
Oakland, while two of us headed in a different direction. I was
in the car leading the way, with Bobby Seale, then chairman of
the Black Panther Party, sitting up front. We had traveled to what
was considered a very dangerous part of town called Hunters
Point in San Francisco. We found ourselves near Victorian homes
in between two industrial buildings. We slipped inside a house
with no lights on, where there were already members waiting.
The fireplace was burning and crackling. As we sat quietly, waiting for the meeting to start, Bobby Seale sat on the stool in front
of the fireplace. As the light flickered off of his body, he looked
around. What came out of his mouth shocked us all.

"The Black Panther Party has been infiltrated by the FBI,"
he informed us. It seemed that his statement had let all of the
oxygen out of the room. He spoke with an alarming voice but
did not reveal any names. He warned us to be careful of who
we spoke to and to be mindful of what we discussed with others

when dealing with Panther business. If there was anyone asking too many questions, we were to report it to headquarters immediately. We had envisioned ourselves as a force who monitored justice in the community. We knew that not all Blacks would be on board with what we were doing, and that was okay. But we hoped that most would see the good we were doing and understand the injustices that we had seen. We witnessed daily the constant police patrol of our neighborhoods, discrimination, and unemployment, and the disdain from those who knew nothing about our lives in the ghetto. We hated that Blacks were killing Blacks as much as anyone. Yet, cracks began to appear in the camaraderie of the Black Panther Party.

If someone dressed in suits and ties, we might call them an Uncle Tom or an Oreo—Black on the outside but white on the inside. But those same folks called us violent troublemakers, hell-bent on selling Black culture out. But we had a new dream, as we felt that Dr. King hadn't gone far enough or deep enough. It was a great dream he had, but just going down the street marching wouldn't get the people with the money to give it up. It wouldn't bring equality and fair opportunities for all. It just annoyed them. It just forced the police to come and make a scene, and then business would continue as usual. The murders, the bad schools, the lack of resources for us . . . it was all just another day's business. This dream was bigger than us. It was bigger than Dr. King—he didn't understand our dream. It was a new way of thinking. Finally, someone realized that we had indeed built this nation. Someone realized that we were a people out of place in time. We had been kidnapped from our homes and made to plant, build, and cultivate this country wage-free—with scars on our backs as payment.

I reported to headquarters one day and was in- **17**
structed to go to a small chapel on West Street in
Oakland. Alone, I arrived outside of the church. As
I approached the front door, I looked down one corner and
saw a Panther posted up standing guard. Looking in the opposite direction, I saw another Panther posted up. I entered the
church only to see a few scattered members in different pews. I
sat in the rear and waited. After about fifteen minutes, the door
behind the pulpit opened. A Panther who I referred to as Big
John came out first, and then another one, and another. To my
surprise, the Prime Minister of the Black Panther Party, Stokely
Carmichael, entered the room after the others. Stokely began
to speak to us about Pan-Africanism—a term I had never heard
before. He said that we of African descent needed to rely on
each other—including those in Africa—for support, as we had
all been exploited. We had all been hurt.

I was so surprised to see Stokely Carmichael, because all of
us in the party knew that there was a hit out on him by both
the police and the FBI. The knowledge of that in itself made
me quite nervous—nervous to the point that my ears became
keener to sound. My eyes were rapidly moving from one side

to the other. Carmichael had been a member of the Student Nonviolent Coordinating Committee, better known as SNCC (pronounced "snick"). This committee contributed to the radical civil rights movement. Carmichael, along with H. Rap Brown and John Lewis, was highly instrumental in the leadership of this organization. Stokely Carmichael had come over to the Black Panther Party along with H. Rap Brown. Carmichael ended up in exile, Brown ended up in prison, and Lewis became a highly respected United States congressman who was a champion for civil rights until his death.

Carmichael spoke to us in a quiet voice explaining pan-African philosophy. As he spoke, I began to understand why pan-African philosophy was important for Black nationalists, Black Panthers, the nonviolent segments of civil rights organizations, and all the civil rights movements starting in Africa, South America, and the Caribbean to know about. We may have all had a different mission statement, but we were all pursuing the same goal: equal access to resources and opportunity. I'm sure this concept frightened the status quo. Because of this, Stokely Carmichael had plenty of reasons to fear for his life. He had the gift of being able to explain systemic racism in such a way that the least educated person in the room would be able to understand it. He would meticulously and vividly paint a clear picture of Blacks' historical plight in this country and around the world. Everyone listening to Carmichael's speech gained a better perception of their personal condition and left the meeting enlightened. I left there wondering why I had been sent to this little chapel with so few members. There was only a room full of quiet whispers from a leader who was certain to be exiled or worse.

Some brothers liked to play basketball, while others liked to wrestle. Some of us had lived in the South, and some were closer to Mexico than the Mason-Dixon Line. None of us had walked the same footpaths, but we all walked in the same shadow of the white establishment. The same went for brothers all over the world. No, I don't mean that every white person everywhere was calling me the N-word. But they didn't have to. The air said it. The water said it. The bathrooms, the roads, the railways, the restaurants, the police, the government, the prisons, the hotels, the pools, and the schools. They all said it. There was a system to the meanness called established conventions, parameters, and boundaries. No wonder we all had a hard time understanding our identity and our worth.

Each of us knew that there were rules but that these rules were not applied equally for all. Sure, we could go into most lunch counters—Dr. Martin Luther King and President Lyndon B. Johnson had helped us with that. Laws, however, could not change the stares, the gaze, the feelings that came from a dozen white folks looking at you. If one of us were to look funny at a white woman, we could end up just like Emmett Till—lynched by a few angry white men who felt that a Black boy had no business sidling up to any pretty white lady, if Emmett even did that. So we watched ourselves. Some folks thought we were angry all the time. I became angry, yes—but not overnight. I became angry after years of watching, hearing, tiptoeing, and playing it safe.

Some people may think that my story is one of radicalization. Some people may think that I had lost my way. No. I decided that instead of watching other people and gauging them to see if I could gain enough "respectability" points, I would find my own way. None of us come without baggage, without a story. We face the world defined not by us, but by a compendium of government and corporate interests. Black communities were not full of citizens, but baggage—obstacles preventing their pet projects. I came with an Oakland story. Those government and corporate people came with the white elite story. I knew the rituals of violence I'd been initiated into. The world of anger had reached so deep that the folks on the outside began to wonder: are Black folks naturally this angry? No, we are not. Anger and rage gave me an avenue for release. Anger and rage gave me permission to shake off the generations of ghettoization imposed upon Black folks. We all struggle in our own way—some of us more successfully than others. When you're at the bottom of the socioeconomic scale, any amount of progress looks pretty good.

My job at the bookstore was going well. All of **18** the white men in their white shirts and ties didn't seem to mind my long natural hair, my Van Dyke mustache, my dark sunglasses, or my leather jacket—and they all knew what my fashion choices represented. It was no secret that I was a member of the Black Panther Party. Many of the young white kids thought it was something exciting. I can only imagine what the suits thought.

There was a guy named Roger who was the manager of the art department in the bookstore. Roger seemed to really take to me for some reason, but I was leery of him because he had a deep Southern accent. My ignorance told me that everyone white from the South hated Black people. I soon found out that I was wrong, and it was quite an education. On a couple of occasions, Roger offered to give me a ride home. At first I refused. But the next time, I took him up on it. We got to our home, and I introduced him to Wanda. He was very nice. We began to talk about world affairs, civil rights, politics, peace, love, and so on. We all agreed on most things.

Roger noticed different artwork hanging around our house. I informed him that it was the work of my girlfriend, Wanda.

He immediately offered her a job, and she accepted. Now, not only did we have more money coming into the household, but Wanda could get art supplies at a discount. This was cause for celebration. We continued to talk, and as we did, I was playing a compilation of music from my jazz collection. I found out that not only was Roger an appreciator of jazz music, but that he was also a piano player. Roger was the gift that kept on giving. We became very close friends, and that's when I realized that my ignorance was something to be ashamed of. Just because the man had a Southern accent didn't mean he was a racist. How stupid could I be? But that had been the extent of my experience and understanding—how many white people have an ignorant understanding of those who are Black based on their experiences?

While listening to my music, Roger heard me make commentary on the songs and about the artists. He asked me if I had ever considered a career as a radio operator. At first I was bewildered.

"Me?" I asked.

"Of course, you!" he responded.

Roger asked me if I would go somewhere with him the coming weekend. I asked him where we were going, but he wouldn't tell me. "Just wait and see," he said. That Saturday morning, he picked me up and we headed for San Francisco. We entered a building with a sign above the doorway that read *KMPX Radio Station*. Roger knew people, and he knew his way about the station. He took me into a production room and began to show me the editing process. He introduced me to the head DJ, who happened to be a Black man. As we talked, I realized that this DJ was a jazz musician—a local drummer I was aware of. Roger became instrumental in my pursuits in the field of radio broadcasting. I began to study for the FCC exam for my license to broadcast.

Oddly enough, a friend's wife who was a UC Berkeley student had received an assignment to be a broadcaster on the local college station, KALX, and was too nervous to be a radio announcer. So, when her husband found out that I was studying for my FCC exam, he suggested that I take over what was to be her programming. And so began my first jazz program, called *Music Anthology*. My program became very popular among the hippies. I got lots of positive feedback. Then the day finally came when I took the FCC exam. It took three hours, but I passed! In a few weeks, I received my FCC license in the mail. I became a legitimate radio operator. That later led to me having a major program on KSAN, a popular station in Berkeley. I also broadcasted as the first announcer on KPOO in San Francisco and also KZSU at Stanford during the holidays. I felt I was using my talents and finding my place in the world.

■ ■ ■ ■ ■ ■ ■

The highest point in my life came when Wanda told me she was pregnant. As our baby grew inside her, I would often sing or scat jazz at Wanda's belly. I wanted our daughter to identify with an American traditional music that came from her people. We prepared Traci for her little sister coming, so when Jinga was born, she was just as excited as we were. Traci always wanted to help with the new baby. She helped change diapers and assisted with feeding. We were a happy family, or so we thought.

With so many positive things happening in my life, I hoped that things would continue on the upward bound. Alas, they did not. Things were beginning to deteriorate in my relationship with Wanda. We both had limited tools to deal with serious committed relationships. We began to drift apart until we eventually split. Simultaneously, tragic things were beginning to take place within the Black Panther Party. I knew of one person who was suspected of being an informant. They tortured and eventually killed the brother. There were rumors all over about members being visited by a goon squad. It was said that people were being beaten up or taken away, never to be seen again.

One day, this sister who had originally tried to recruit me told me a story about a member in high standing in the party. Not only was he in good standing, but he was a very close friend of Eldridge Cleaver's, as they had been in the penitentiary together. She reminded me of the night in Hunters Point after the rally. Bobby Seale had revealed that the infiltrators of the Black Panther Party were from the FBI. She pointed out to me the place where Cleaver allegedly stayed. His next-door neighbor was his good friend—and an informant. In fact, this informant was the one who had revealed that Cleaver and some of the other Panthers were smuggling weapons the night that Bobby Hutton was shot and killed. She also told me that the Panthers had arranged for an informant who was also present at the shooting to go underground. His location was in Seattle, Washington, under the protection of the Seattle chapter of the Black Panthers. The member in question had never been seen again. She led me to believe that during his relocation, he had been executed. My loss of Wanda's love and my loss of faith in the Black Panther Party sent me into an emotional and mental whirlwind. The places I thought I had found purpose and belonging—a community, a family—were crumbling apart.

I began to medicate myself with alcohol and more drugs. I no longer affiliated myself with the Black Panther Party. There was much talk of extortion from merchants all over Oakland by the Black Panthers. In other words, pay for protection—just like the days of Al Capone. The entire Bay Area was flooded with cocaine. Cocaine changed the rules, cocaine changed the vision, and cocaine destroyed the movement.

After such disappointment, loss, and sorrow, my anger was at an all-time high. Before our breakup, Wanda had wanted to move to a larger place with more room. I didn't think we were financially ready for that, but Wanda was very insistent. So, I had agreed to move with her. We found a nice house at the end of a cul-de-sac with a creek in the backyard in East Oakland. Once there, though, we had seemed to drift even further apart. Wanda had more than just good looks—she had artistic talent and the ability to see things as they really were. She had a way with people, and she definitely had a way with me. And now she was gone. I had to move on, or else I would shrink into nothingness.

A friend of mine had also had a breakup with his girlfriend, and he suggested that we get a cool bachelor pad together. We found a great three-bedroom apartment at the top of a hill in a good neighborhood in Oakland, and so it began. Parties, wine, women, and song. Oh, and I forgot—drugs also. It was a hollow kind of life.

It was sometimes a struggle to keep from thinking about how much worse off my life was by being without Wanda. I centered my attention on the drug trade simply because work didn't keep me busy enough or give me enough money. When you have something that everybody wants, they're always glad to see you. I needed to be needed, to feel that I mattered to someone—a longing I'd had so many other times in my life. I would get a lot of people asking about other things to get high on. I already had a decent marijuana clientele, but it was small-time now. The thing that was in demand was cocaine, and I had access to both quality and quantity. I no longer had to concern myself with taking chances because I was only worrying about myself now—it was me against the world.

My trust level in relationships was very low. Not just with women, but with everything and everyone. When it came to people, I could be physically all in, but not emotionally. I did not believe that I could ever find another romantic relationship. I didn't know if it mattered.

I was taking music classes at Merritt College, but my drug lifestyle was taking up most of my time. Drugs and the constant connections I had to maintain for them interfered with my schoolwork.

I looked at my job at the bookstore as an opportunity to create a larger customer base. I treated it as a time to network and create better connections for myself. After all, we were in Berkeley. I became more and more engaged with whites. I involved them in trafficking cocaine. Cocaine soon became my principal concern. I became influential in many people's lives—but not for the better. Some hadn't even encountered cocaine before they met me. Soon I was also becoming a witness to some of their lives being destroyed. The influence of drugs on people is overwhelming, and I reaped the financial benefits of their destruction before moving on to the next victim. I also became my own best customer, which was the beginning of my demise as a human being.

In 1983, an opportunity arose for me to relocate to another job in Hawaii, which was exciting. I moved to Hawaii with a friend who also had a job there. The local people were very hospitable. I became the inventory coordinator for eighteen stores that specialized in leisure and junior sportswear. It was a management position, but Hawaiian jobs didn't pay as well as California jobs. I wanted to live as well as I did in California. Hawaii was a lot more expensive.

In reality, I was running from my addiction and running from all of the sorrow that I had caused. Though there was beauty all around me, most of the time, I walked around with a very heavy and sad heart. In spite of the smile on my face, I was not a happy person. What made it even worse was the day I was approached by my boss and found out he was a cocaine dealer. He was the production manager for the entire company I worked for, but he was also the coke man for the company. He wanted me to have a sample of his product. It didn't take me long to get back into the swing of things. Before I knew it, I was working just to pay off my cocaine debt to him. I didn't have a clientele like I'd had on the mainland. I couldn't sell for profit or manage my addiction. I was trapped.

One day, someone suggested to me that I watch a program on TV. They didn't tell me anything about it, but they believed that it would help **20** me. The following morning, I did just that. I turned on the program, and lo and behold, it was about the forgiveness of Jesus Christ. I remember listening intently to the message of love they were conveying to everyone listening. I found it difficult to reconcile the possibility and reality that Jesus loved me when I didn't love myself. Why would Jesus love *me*? I continued to listen to people share their testimonies. Before I knew it, I was sobbing. On the TV screen, they presented a phone number to call. In the midst of my despair, I called that number. The woman on the other end of the phone asked for my address. I gave it to her, and that was the end of the conversation. Little did I know, they were sending someone out right away.

I lived in Kaimuki, above Honolulu. At Waikiki overlooking Diamondhead, at the foot of that mountain, was a Baptist church in the midst of a revival. Even though the broadcast I had been watching was located somewhere on the mainland, they had a networking system with local churches. When someone called that number, they would have a Christian church somewhere nearby answer the call of the person in distress. Soon, there were three men at my door. As they approached, I heard them talking. Two of the men had Southern accents, which was strange to me at the time. It almost made me not want to answer the door. But something made me go and open the door and allow them to come in.

As they began to minister about the forgiveness of Christ to me, they offered to pray for me. They encouraged me to repeat what they referred to as the sinner's prayer. As I repeated the words after them, the tears began to flow once again. It was like there was a cleansing taking place. It gave me a feeling of gratitude as a burden lifted from my entire being. The light of Christ was touching my soul. Afterwards, they invited me to come to their revival the following evening, and I agreed. When that time came, though, I found myself wrestling with whether I should go or not. I overcame my trepidation and went.

As I listened to all of the scriptures and heard them say how much God wanted to have a relationship with us, it felt like it was a message from God directly to me. I was offered the opportunity to be baptized in the name of Jesus Christ. I remember feeling very nervous but also happy at the same time. That following Sunday, I was about to be baptized for the second time in my life. I hadn't really understood the first time as a child, and I don't really know if I totally understood what I was doing this time. I do know that I felt something that I had never thought would exist between me, Jesus Christ, and our Heavenly Father. After being baptized, I felt like I had a new lease on life. Not many of the members spoke to me, except the pastor, his sister, and a handful of church members. We became good friends. I was now what they called "born again."

■ ■ ■ ■ ■ ■ ■

For the first time in a while, I had a good feeling. It was a little odd to me at first. It seemed that I felt peace with all that was around me. Peace with birds, cats, dogs, even the plants. However, I didn't feel like I had direction, besides being advised by the pastor to read and study the word of God. I had read through the Bible from Genesis to Revelation. Much of it was enlightening, but there were many things I didn't understand. It never dawned on me to pray and ask God for wisdom, knowledge, or understanding. I just read it like I was reading a novel. I have to admit—it helped me a lot in terms of obedience. However, I felt that I was not applying myself enough.

I began to approach the word of God with an attitude of searching. I didn't understand what the scriptures meant about garments, or Aaron's priesthood, or how these things could apply to me. I didn't understand the devices that Exodus referred to as the Urim and Thummim. There were a lot of important references to the temple of the Lord, which made me wonder why this had never been an important topic in all of the different churches I had been to. None of the denominations I had been exposed to really discussed it. Scripture tells us that the Lord is the same yesterday, today, and always. So, what about this *temple* stuff? Does each church have secrets pertaining to their own temples? Maybe you had to be of high stature in order to know the answers to these secrets. Who was Melchizedek? He appears in Hebrews. What was this office of priest? Were they talking about Catholic priests? I didn't think so. I thought Jesus Himself was nondenominational. At least, I hoped He was—even though I was attending a Southern Baptist church in

Hawaii. I was finding some answers, but they often led to more questions.

I certainly didn't understand everything, and those were just a few things that puzzled me within the word of God. Of course, some things were too lofty for me, but wasn't I supposed to generally understand—or be taught by someone who did? Regardless, the things I understood made me feel good, and isn't that what the Bible was supposed to do? Make people feel good? Somehow, I was looking for the Bible to give me some guidelines on how I was to survive this world by myself. Little did I understand that I wasn't supposed to do it by myself. That understanding didn't come during this part of my journey.

．．．．．．．．

I thought about the different things that were in my life that I should stop doing—a lot of which I wasn't sure about. One of those questions was how music would fit into my new life. One day after church, my new friend Robert's brother-in-law approached me. In his pidgin accent, he asked, "Eddie, you like da kine music, brah?" I told him that I loved music. I did not know if I should play any music other than Christian. I explained to him that I played a little flute, but I was mostly interested in pursuing percussion instruments like conga drums, bongos, Agogo bells, tambourine, and other instruments from South America, Africa, or the Caribbean. He explained to me that he was involved in a contemporary Christian band and asked if I was interested in checking them out. I joyfully accepted the offer. There was a Chinese female singer and guitar player, a Portuguese bass player, a Caucasian engineer, a Hawaiian drummer, and now an African American percussionist. We became the group called David Psalm. The drummer and I attended our church, while the bass player, engineer, and lead singer attended a different church. Our aim was to use our music to minister the gospel to those who did not know the Lord Jesus.

One day, after a rehearsal of some new songs, **21** the members of our band were headed for our respective vehicles. Out in front, we saw some young white men approaching. They wore white shirts, ties, and name badges. It looked as if they were going to greet me, but the group stopped me from saying anything. In loud voices, they shouted, "Yo, Eddie, don't talk to them, brother!" I asked them why. In pidgin, one of them said, "Oh! Day da kine one cult brah!"

"What? What kind of cult?" I asked.

"Day da kine Mormon, brah," he said.

"What do they do?" I asked.

"Oh! We don't know."

So, I didn't return the young men's greeting. I did think that it was weird and rude, but I let it go.

■ ■ ■ ■ ■ ■ ■

Something different about living in Hawaii was that the local people would often discriminate against whites. There was a lot of betrayal and broken promises in the history between whites and Hawaiians. I thought my friends' reaction to these people called Mormons had something to do with that. A white person would need to have a different attitude and behavior for the locals to befriend or trust them.

We played music all over the island. To my surprise, we received many invitations to play. After attending our respective churches on Sunday, we would go to Waikiki Beach and sing to many vacationers and beachgoers that had partied all weekend. It was a very fulfilling ministry—some indeed received the Lord Jesus Christ because of us.

We gained some local fame, and I started getting invitations to play with other groups. The first band the drummer and I played with was another Christian collective, but then I got invited to play with a Hawaiian band known as the Brothers Ho'okipa. My phone rang off the hook with invitations to play, and I was having a really good time doing it. I even played with the Don Ho Band.

One day during lunch I was walking on the grounds of the company I worked for. A dreadlocked brother spoke to me, asking if I was Ed Willis. "Are you Maacho?" I asked. I had heard about this man, a reggae musician. He worked for the same company I did. After a brief conversation, he asked if I would be interested in meeting him at Rendezvous Studios to hear the material that his band wanted to record. I accepted the offer to meet up with him the upcoming Tuesday evening. Upon my arrival, he introduced me to a Frenchman who was the owner and engineer of the studio. They had a booth set up for me with headphones, and I brought my own conga drums. Maacho instructed me to play along with the music I was hearing in the headphones. The music was this dynamic and beautiful reggae music. As the music played, I played. After the second song, he asked me if I wanted to be a member of the band. Of course!

I was all over the island playing music with different bands. However, the more music I played, the less scripture I read. The more clubs I played in, the less church I attended. After becoming born again, I didn't stop drinking alcohol. Since playing with these bands, I began to drink more than before. In no way am I blaming the bands for my lack of focus in church. It wasn't the bands' fault, nor the church's fault. Being in those situations exposed me to a lot of marijuana and cocaine as well. Before I knew it, I was no longer attending church.

I soon began to use drugs at work with my boss and fellow employees. I even began to use drugs with the bands I was playing with. One day, I was leaving a local boy's house after smoking marijuana. As I sped down the highway, listening to loud music, an even louder voice yelled, "EDDIE WILLIS!!!!" It was so loud that it frightened me to the point where I had to pull over and turn the music down. I broke out in a cold sweat, shaking and wondering what had happened—wondering if I was going nuts. I couldn't understand how such a thing could happen. I thought that it could have been the effects of the drugs, but a strong sense of fear came over me when I considered the possibility that it could have been the Lord. Talk about being spooked—I was spooked to the tenth degree. After the shakes stopped, I merged slowly back on the road toward home.

■ ■ ■ ■ ■ ■ ■

Things didn't get better—they got worse. That local boy I mentioned became my roommate. Some days, I would come home from work and he would be cooking a large cafeteria pot full of cocaine.

An interesting chain of events began to take place—and it

all changed everything. For recreation, I liked boogie boarding and bodysurfing. One day, at Makapu'u Pool, I was bodysurfing in an area with too many people also bodysurfing. I injured my neck that day, which caused me great pain.

The following weekend, I was in Kane'ohe Bay on a catamaran that capsized in water full of hammerhead sharks. After going under, my life jacket forced me up with such speed that I hit my head on the catamaran. I was nearly knocked out. I soon realized where I was—being circled by hammerhead sharks—and immediately collected myself. I climbed on the bottom of the boat as it was facing upward.

The next weekend, I went to Laie's North Shore, which was known for its twenty-foot waves. This was a popular spot for expert surfers. I went in with my trusty boogie board. As I caught a good-sized wave, I felt a piercing pain in my right ankle. I looked toward it and saw the emerald-colored water change to blood red. I thought of sharks immediately. It was *my* blood, and the pain was intense. In an instant, I felt as if there were a mighty hand that had grabbed a hold of my left ankle. With much strength, it pulled me down and back away from the shore. This was my experience with what they called an undertow. I knew I was in for the fight of my life. I began to fight with all that I had. During this fight, I saw pieces of sharp coral in the water, which let me know the cause of my injury. My fight would intensify after each tug from underneath the water. I soon began to win. Finally, I made it to shore. Gasping for breath, I looked down at my bloody ankle and realized how close to death's door I really had been. That was my last time going in the water in Hawaii. After pondering these events, I realized that these were signs for me to go.

Before moving to Hawaii, I had thought that I would only

be staying for two years maximum, but the two years had turned into over six. It was now June 1989. I'd had a safeguard put in place that whenever I needed to leave, I had the money set aside for a plane ticket to return to the mainland. I borrowed the company truck and handed out all my stuff to different local families and friends. I even gave one local boy and his family my car—for free. I got off the island right away.

I stayed with a friend in San Francisco and **22** took a few days to recoup. My friend suggested that I get a job there, but I didn't feel that San Francisco was the place I wanted to be. I decided that I would go to the East Bay—the Berkeley and Oakland side of the bay. Each day, my friend would go to work, and I would use the car to go over to the East Bay and visit friends I hadn't seen in a while. When I was still living in Hawaii, my mother had informed me that my brother Kevin was dying of cancer. I knew he was sick before I left, but there were stages when he seemed better. From the sound of my mother's voice now, I could tell that I needed to get there right away. I spent my first week home with my brother. I did not let the rest of my family or anyone else know that I was in town. I just wanted that time with my brother.

Kevin was at a hospital in San Francisco, and I'd visit him every morning. After my brother passed, I went into a stupor. I was getting wrecked on dope. Kevin was a good kid—he never got into trouble like me, his big brother. He was in Alameda Junior College, was good at tennis, and was working. He had a beautiful girlfriend, who I believe was thinking of marriage.

When I moved back to the mainland, I was more open to all of the new changes going on. Things had gone really wild in the six years that I was gone. Now, you could get about anything you wanted if you had crack cocaine. Everyone had gone absolutely nuts for this drug. It didn't take me long to realize that I needed to get a job really quickly or else I would never be able to be at the top of the food chain.

■ ■ ■ ■ ■ ■ ■

I once again became a functioning addict. I got jobs, but I couldn't keep them. I started with a good-paying job for an engineering supply company. However, the more money I made, the more I invested into my illness. Food became a luxury. Each draw from a crack pipe sends you deeper into the oblivion, an abyss where everyone has their own bottom. Many try to hold on to or even fake their humanity, but no one can for long. I tried to fake my humanity myself.

Addiction opens you up to witnessing all kinds of literal and figurative death. Death in relationships between husbands and wives. Deaths among siblings. Death of character, death of morals. Some of these deaths are inflicted upon others, while some are self-inflicted. Addiction places you in the lion's den, with humans that prey on other humans like animals. I will not share the individual horrors that I witnessed or was a part of. There did come a time when I no longer had the resources or money that I'd had before. The loss of my job, the loss of respect for myself, and the loss of respect for others took its toll. As usual, it was nighttime and I was in another person's home. When I ran out of drugs, this person became verbally abusive. A fight ensued. Shortly after this fight, I got into two more physical altercations. At this point, I had a limp and was very hurt. I tried to gain refuge in several different places, but no one would allow me to enter. Rejected, I felt the only place I could go home to was my parents' house.

I had a bus ticket that would get me there. My parents lived two blocks and around a corner from the bus stop, where I was let off. Because of the pain I was in, it felt like I had walked two miles. It was late—at least 3:00 a.m.—but fortunately, I had a key. When I attempted to unlock the door, I discovered my key no longer worked. I knocked and knocked but still received no answer. I went to my parents' bedroom window and tapped there until my dad's voice said, "Eddie, go away!" The heartbreak I felt at these words was, and still is, ineffable. I cannot express the inner pain that those words brought. That pain turned into an angry rage—so much that my father called the police. The police found me outside cursing at my dad, which I had never done before. The police gave me an ultimatum: either leave or go to jail.

At that statement, I heard my mother plead with me, "Eddie, please leave."

With that, I walked away sad and dejected. As I walked around the corner, the reality dawned on me that no one wanted or cared about me, so I wept. I remembered that in my parents' backyard, there was a broken-down van without doors. I took refuge there for the rest of that morning, cold and alone in tears of pain. This was the end of my road. How was I to survive? I got up the nerve to pray. After daylight, I humbly went back to my parents' door and knocked. Daddy let me in, but he didn't say a word. I asked to use the phone, and my mother said yes with tears in her eyes. I could see the pain that my choices had brought her.

I told a friend about my situation, and he agreed to let me stay at his house with his family. I collected a few belongings, and my dad gave me a ride to Piedmont, a very nice community where my friend stayed. He suggested that I attend a recovery program for drug addiction. I didn't know such a thing existed. I didn't know that there was a place for anyone to get help from this insanity. I had come home on June 6, 1989, and by November 6, 1989, I was down and out. Thus, my road to recovery began when I was accepted into a Christian recovery program. It lasted a full year. I also ended up on staff in that program, which added another year plus. After that, I got help from the administrator to be a resident in a men's Christian organization. This organization was comprised of men who had successfully graduated out of year-long programs.

I would like to tell you that it was all a successful story from then on, but I can't. Over the next decade, there were lots of failures and some successes. I became a personal banker, and later an administrator for a corporation. Yet, I didn't want to believe some things, I didn't want to trust some things, and I didn't want to give up some things. Some things were triggers to my addiction. Some people were triggers to my addiction. Until I had the strength and conviction to withstand any outside influences, I would always be on this roller-coaster ride.

I got a job in 2004 with the Men of Valor, which was a Christian organization developed by the Acts Full Gospel Church. This organization helped ex-cons and men on their way to prison for drug-related offenses. It was a campus environment—everything was provided there. It was a good-paying job, and it was very fulfilling working with these men. I got to witness their confidence growing and see them hope for a different life. Still, I was not ready for a full, meaningful life myself. I was just going through the motions—I didn't feel like there was purpose for my life.

There were times when I would visit my mother at her senior citizens' apartment where she was living. I would cook, clean, and keep her company as we would talk and watch television. One night, she became so despondent and ill to the point that I called the ambulance. As they took my mother to the hospital, I was concerned but not fearful. My fear came after four days passed and my mother did not return home. It was a blur to me how many days had passed before I finally had the conversation with my sister in which she told me that our mother had died.

At first, I didn't believe it. I didn't believe that my mother was no longer going to be there to support me no matter how bad I had gotten. I didn't believe that in spite of all that had happened in the past, she was never again going to be there to laugh with me, talk with me, encourage me, or console me. It didn't take long for reality to set in, however. I was no longer going to have my mother to lean on. My mother was truly gone from the picture of my life. My sister Karen handled all of the

From left to right: Karen, Kevin, my mother (Mazie), me, and Frank, 1978

arrangements for the funeral. It was small, but everyone who attended said something loving about my mother. It was all true. Everyone loved my mother, because my mother had time to listen to everyone. Happy or sad, you could talk to Mazie Willis.

How strange it was that my mother had died a year and five months after my little brother Frank had passed away. Kevin was already gone, and my stepfather too. Only my sister Karen and I remain today. I couldn't help but feel empty, more than I had ever felt before. I was familiar with that empty feeling. A tremendous emptiness had come at the end of my relationship with Wanda, and it was back again upon my mother's death. Two major women in my life—gone. My mother had been my rock. She always prayed for me. I couldn't help but realize just how small the family had gotten.

■ ■ ■ ■ ■ ■ ■

It was just Karen and me. Karen had her hands full with two growing girls, a household to run, a job to keep, and a church to do work for. There wasn't much room for me. I had to find my own place in this life. From the time of my mother's death, I could do nothing but reflect on days gone by . . . all of the experiences, challenges, wrong decisions, adventures, and yes—sins.

I thought about all of my attempts at success. Even while I was doing my best at my various jobs, I was addicted to so many things that were unhealthy. In my world, being employed had meant that you were able to pay your own way for drugs, alcohol, or any other poison of your choice. You could pay for your own death.

All that I reflected on in my life was mere waste— meaningless tripe. As my mind raced through time, I reflected on how my perception of things had changed over time. When I was in the Black Panther Party, I seemed to gain a form of dignity and purpose with a sense of hope for myself and my people. However, I realized that I had lifted man up a little too high. In other words, I thought man could resolve the inner turmoil that was within me, and I unfairly assigned that responsibility to the leaders of the Black Panther Party. After all, they were *only* men, and they were also dealing with their own inner turmoil.

All of my failed ventures led to a life of disgrace—disgrace that brought shame with drugs, alcohol, and bad behavior.

Everybody has their own bottom, and I was at mine. No, I was not eating out of garbage cans, at least not yet. No, I was not robbing innocent people at gunpoint for my own survival. But I was no better than anyone who did these things. I was truly at my wits' end. I wasn't currently using drugs, but I wondered what tomorrow would bring. I wondered if I would ever be honest with myself. Fear was at my doorstep, and all hope could have been lost if I didn't find my way toward a better means of living.

There have been times in my life when I knew people who chose the way of suicide. I thought of how desperate or destitute people who committed suicide must have been emotionally. Was I there now? I reflected on my emotional state, only to find out that I lacked the conviction to carry that out. In my twisted place of anguish, I somehow viewed suicide as an act of courage. Again, I asked myself why I had done so many courageous things in my life, only to find out that I was a coward. During this vigorous self-inventory, I could only come up with dark answers, if any answers at all.

■ ■ ■ ■ ■ ■ ■

The event of my mother's death caused me to do some serious reflection on my life. Perhaps for the first time, I was honest with myself in admitting that I was disappointed in the way my life was turning out and the person that I had become. I couldn't see any rewards in simply being clean and sober—that in itself would not lead to the blessings and fulfillment of purpose I hoped for. And that was a dangerous way to feel. If I threw in the towel and gave in fully to my vices, it would be a death warrant. I was feeling that there was nothing to live for. What could I possibly do? I was in a place of despair.

After much pondering, the reality of how bad things truly were finally hit me. I came to the realization that if I wanted to be happier and have a fulfilled life, then God had to be at the forefront of my life. That realization hit me powerfully, and it moved me to cry out to God in a sincere prayer of repentance that brought on gut-wrenching tears.

"Oh, my God!" I pled in prayer. Was this the end of me? Had I received so many accolades from so many people, only to find out how meaningless everything really was? I wanted to live, but how could I go on? "Lord, help me!" I cried audibly, with no one else around. Again I invoked His name, and yet could it be possible that He heard? Was there a chance? Even now, I remember that force welling up in my chest, beads of sweat beginning to form on my forehead, sweaty palms, and quivering knees. How many times had I turned my back on God? How many times had I chosen my way over His way? How many times had I betrayed Jesus Christ? Throughout my life, I had been told time and time again that Christ was standing there waiting for me at the door, and I chose not to open it. Dare I even ask for life, for another chance?

I found myself speaking out loud as if someone were there with me. Then, I cried out in a louder voice, "God, forgive me, please! In the name of Jesus Christ!" I cannot remember how long I went on. But, as I wept, my whole body became warm. As I sobbed, a sense of nurturing, a feeling of me being loved permeated my entire existence. It was as if some unseen power had reached into my heart to soothe all the burdens that I had carried for so many years. There was something reaching deep inside me. I surmised, in my finite thinking, that it could only be God Himself. This realization caused me to cry even more, but they were now tears of joy—a joy I had never felt until that day. Yes, I'd laughed, I'd had fun, but this was not the same. This was deeper, richer, real and everlasting.

I firmly believe with every breath that I take that that time was the beginning of a transition point in my life, and the reality of God's love for me was coming to fruition. I could feel it inside my soul, and there was no denying it. The wave of repentance that came over me culminated in an elated feeling that there was a loving presence there that embraced me. I knew that it was God. No one could ever say anything to convince me otherwise. I was alone in the room physically, but there was something greater than me that was giving me an embrace of love and caring and nurturing.

"I am not worthy," I said. So many thoughts washed over me in a rush. *What an utter fool I've been*, I thought. This magnificent love, grace, and mercy had been available to me all that time, and I'd had blinders on. I was blinded to the truth. My mom had made me go to Sunday school and taught me to pray, but those had just been gestures. This loving embrace from God was real, and it penetrated to the very heart of me. I felt that there were no restrictions for me there in the arms of God's love. There were neither economics, nor systems, nor philosophies that could keep me from the liberty that waited for me through Jesus Christ. He was truly sending light to my mind, joy to my heart, and freedom to my soul.

From that time forth, I could feel deeply that the Spirit of God was with me. Everyone's story of coming to know the Lord is different, and for many, faith comes slowly, by degrees, with periods of doubt in between. But as for me, at no time after that prayer of repentance did I ever feel any doubt that the Lord was with me and that He was going to guide me out of my despair. The joy of knowing that stayed with me, and I sometimes felt that I might be walking around with almost a smirk on my face, because I felt like I knew a secret that a lot of people didn't know.

I always felt that during this transition period the Lord was with me on a greater level than we might typically feel. There was an undoubting, absolute confidence that no matter what, the power of God was with me. He had a specific plan for me, and that plan was going to be greater than anything I could have ever possibly imagined for myself (and I've had some really vain imaginations!). The mystery and excitement of that filled my heart with joy.

It was very difficult to contain myself at this point. I looked around feverishly to see who else was witnessing this metamorphosis. I know I **24** must have looked very animated during this change the Lord had put me through, because I found myself on the ground. I had started on my feet. I could barely contain myself—what must I do now? I decided to start by taking deep breaths to calm the beating of my heart. An interesting sense seemed to be trying to penetrate this feeling of new life. Doubts came, telling me that my sins and crimes of wickedness could never be forgiven. I was afraid that these feelings of elation would pass. I recognized that this was the enemy from darkness and lies, so I immediately rebuked it. I began to think about some of the ownership I had to take for the things I'd done to gratify my flesh.

I humbly asked the Lord in prayer to help me to be sensitive to His leading, for I did not know what direction to go in, or even what church to attend. That night, I began to get the sense that God wanted me to just be patient, wait, and follow the promptings I'd receive. From that time on, everything that happened in my life was glory after glory after glory. The Lord was setting me on His path and taking me out of my circumstances not only emotionally but geographically. One of His glories came in the form of a phone call. After many days of scripture reading, studying, and meditating, I was called to the phone by one of my housemates. My sister was on the phone with good news. Karen was about to embark on a trip to Southern California with her two daughters to visit Wanda and her family members. Wanda, her sister Elva, and my granddaughter Alina all lived together. Our daughters, Traci and Jinga, also lived in Southern California in the Los Angeles area.

Before I could think, I asked Karen to call Wanda and ask if it would be all right if I joined them. Wanda had invited me to come visit family just before my mother passed away. Karen agreed that I should go and hung up the phone to call Wanda. I felt a certain level of excitement. In about fifteen minutes, the phone rang again. It was Karen, who told me that I was indeed welcome to visit them in Southern California with her. I didn't know how long the trip would be, nor did I care. Interestingly, I had no concerns at all about my well-being. I didn't have a job, but I had no concerns about it. I had no concerns about money. I had no concerns about whether my health was going to hold up. I knew that my future was being provided for by the Lord, and whatever was going to happen would be according to His will. And it was! Every single thing—including my trip to Southern California.

· · · · · · · ·

The time had come for our departure, which was before dawn. I didn't take much—only a few clothes and my Bible. I slept most of the way. It was one of the best slumbers I'd had in a long time. When I wasn't asleep, I was engaged in joyful conversation with my sister and nieces. They were also excited about the trip. I have to admit there were times I couldn't help but wonder how I would be received by Wanda. Then the thought came to me: she had not seen the broken man that I had become. She and all of the others would only be seeing the man that the Lord was putting back together.

We went up a street with a steep incline in somewhat of an upper-middle-class neighborhood. I began to get a little nervous as we pulled up to the home where Wanda lived, feeling anxious about how they would receive me. With a deep breath, I knocked on the door. When Wanda opened the door, we were all greeted with hugs—and I mean *real* hugs, the ones with meaning! Wanda looked well, as she seemed legitimately excited to see me. Then Elva entered the room with her great smile and welcoming words. The house was lovely, and it carried a sweet feeling of joy, happiness, and peace. Wanda had been in the Church of Jesus Christ for some time, so the Spirit was present in her home. There's a meekness you sense in many disciples of Christ, and I sensed this in Wanda. It was very comforting and welcoming to be received that way in her household. There was nothing making me apprehensive or nervous; I was fully comfortable in her home.

While staying in Wanda's home, I was encouraged inwardly to stay in touch with the Lord through prayer and scripture reading. I wasn't trying to convince anybody else that I had become a better man or persuade anybody to think differently of me—it simply was essential to my survival, and to surviving the way God wanted me to. I knew that the way I could stay sensitive to His promptings was to frequently be in prayer and be in scripture. I would use quiet times in the mornings to pray and study because I did not want to lose the marvelous gift I had gained—the presence of the Lord Jesus in my life. I took each morning as an opportunity to meet with my Heavenly Father through Christ Jesus. I would kneel and thank Him for His love, His mercy, and for the new life I could feel growing inside me. Little did I know, Wanda was able to look down from the upstairs railing and see my morning dedication with the Lord. Eventually I found out I was being observed. It turned out that this was a good observation. Wanda later shared with me that who she saw was not the Eddie she had once known.

This was just the beginning. One night, after a wonderful dinner, I remember asking if there was any brandy in the house. "I'm sorry. We do not drink in this house," Wanda replied. For an instant, I was being subject to the flesh without even a second thought. I learned that night that my spirit must become stronger than the urges of my flesh. At the time of my request to Wanda, I'd had no thought or idea that alcohol was in any way going to be contrary to where my spirit was being led.

Upon finding out about our arrival, our youngest daughter Jinga arrived happy and full of joy to see all of us. That included me, the absentee father I'd been for quite some time. This was something I didn't know how to fix, but Jinga was full of smiles and laughter because I was there now. We also met Wanda's close friend, who made the comment that she and I looked alike. I commented that Wanda and I were soul mates. Other than my immediate family, Wanda was my first real adult experience with domestic life.

A lot of my firsts had come with Wanda. I'd never had a lamb chop until Wanda. I'd never had a filet mignon until Wanda. I had never even had a German chocolate cake until Wanda. Of course, these were just minor things. Our bond in our earlier years was impressive to most, even to the point of jealousy by many. We had built the structure of a home and a family at such an early age. Many of our friends who were our age had not been ready for such a commitment. Yes, we were soul mates. Some people called us Bonnie and Clyde. Neither of us seemed to have jelled with anyone else as closely as we had with one another. We were now both single and had not married. Throughout my life, there were times when I would have a recurring dream of myself in a domestic setting with a wife and family who loved me. I would wake up from this dream in a cold sweat, as if it were a nightmare. In fact, it was something I desired. However, I could not believe that an existence like that could ever be available to me.

All good things must come to an end, and it
was time to head back toward the San Francisco
Bay area. Even though we were departing, I had
a feeling that I had been incorporated into Wanda's family. I no
longer had to feel alone.

When I arrived in San Francisco, I immediately continued
my spiritual regimen of scripture study and prayer, and I began
having phone conversations with Wanda every night. I wanted
to keep myself intact and keep the presence of the Lord's Spirit
in my life. I was staying in a lucrative area of San Francisco
called Bernal Heights, house-sitting for a friend. They had provided plenty of alcohol for me, and I had always enjoyed good
wine. One night on the phone, in a weak defense of my actions,
I said to Wanda that Jesus also drank wine. Wanda immediately
replied that no man of hers would be partaking of the grape in
that manner.

It then occurred to me that drinking alcohol might interfere with my relationship with the Lord, and it definitely would
interfere with my relationship with Wanda. I decided to quit
drinking. This led me to next feel inspired to give up cigarettes.
The thought came to me that my smoking habit could also be

interfering with my relationship with the Lord. I threw away my last two cigarettes and never bought another pack. After pondering these things, I also decided to give up coffee. I loved strong, imported coffee and had a habit of drinking it frequently. But I had no more desire to continue succumbing to these substances, even though I knew they might come back as temptations.

I decided right then, after years of drinking alcohol and coffee and smoking, that I wouldn't do any of those things anymore. Even though my house was stocked with plenty of alcohol that I enjoyed, I would drink no more. In reality, I was more intrigued by a renewed relationship with the Lord and with Wanda than I was by any of those drinks. The strange thing was that I didn't experience any withdrawals from any of them, nor did I struggle with denying myself any of these habitual desires. My quest in the Lord and the possibility of a new life with Wanda were more powerful than any of those substances.

Needless to say, this was a freedom I really could not explain. There was no longer a five-hundred-pound yoke wrapped around my neck. Instead, there was now another stage of freedom the Lord had gifted me with on my journey. I do know that the Spirit of the Lord was the only reason why this miracle happened. The only explanation for my ability to overcome my addictions was that the Lord was with me and strengthening me. In no way could I have done this on my own, and yet I still felt that more blessings were yet to come. The Lord was sending me the message that once I repented, I was in His hands. I was bought and paid for. The Lord was clearing the path for me to find the fullness of His truth.

During this time of seeking the Lord, I visited many churches. They were all full of wonderful people, but they seemed to fall short of what the Bible said the Church should be.

I didn't quite feel the wholeness I was seeking. I kept praying to Heavenly Father in the name of Jesus Christ, along with fasting, meditating, and studying, all on my own. I asked God to lead me to others who were like-minded and who followed Him.

■ ■ ■ ■ ■ ■ ■

Wanda and I spoke of many things during our nightly conversations, including the topic of marriage. In fact, we both expressed the desire to be married. We discussed our failed relationships over the years. During our conversations, we always remained friendly toward one another. We eventually admitted to each other that deep down, we had not totally lost the feelings we'd had for one another. They were just buried deep inside.

Wanda also expressed to me that she and her sister Elva had been moved to send me some money as a form of a tithe. The next morning, I was to go to Western Union to receive this blessing that Wanda and Elva had sent for me. This was just one more way that the Lord was meeting my needs and guiding my path through His servants.

I recall one day pondering scripture and feeling the joy and freedom that the words of truth provided for my inner and outer self. I began to see things differently. My mind skipped to a memory of earnest prayer beside my bed one night. I had been a member of a men's Christian organization located in West Oakland in the early nineties. I remembered being in a state of fervent prayer, expressing to the Lord that in my innermost self, I felt that I would one day be free of the struggle with my vices. As I began to express my inability to find the strength to overcome them myself, I pled so hard for help that it brought tears to my eyes. I cried with so much intensity that I began to gasp

for breath. I remembered that after that fervent prayer, I continued to kneel and sob. At the time, my tears were those of defeat.
Now, I actually felt free from all of these bondages. With the
small portion of wisdom I seemed to have gained, I realized that
there were bondages deep within me that I must confront also.

■ ■ ■ ■ ■ ■ ■

The time had come for me to get back to the east side of
the bay, where my sister had agreed to allow me to stay with
her. While there, I was to pursue employment leads I had set up
before our trip to Southern California. Strangely, both job prospects fell through. I made all of the necessary calls, arrived at all
of my appointments on time, yet those who were supposed to
be on the other end never showed up. On the fourth day, I came
back from an appointment where I was supposed to receive res-
idency. The person that I was to meet had not come to the
appointment. I began to return to my sister's house only to run
into two characters I knew from my dark days. I could see they
had been up all night. These two men were gangsters who had
always had my back. When they saw how I looked, they broke
out with smiles of joy, only to follow up with a plea for money.
"Hey," one of them said, "do you have any change or money
that you could help us out with?" I reached into my pocket and
handed them fifteen dollars. They ran off jumping for joy.

I realized then that there was nowhere I could possibly be in
the Bay Area and not encounter someone that was still living in
the dark. In other words, I would always run into someone from
my past. I decided that I would no longer pursue job prospects
there. I also decided that I would begin thinking of new options
to pursue during my nightly conversations with Wanda, which

were extremely uplifting spiritually. I began to convey to her the challenges that I was having in pursuing what I thought had been sure things.

"Why don't you move down here and get a job?" Wanda replied.

"I don't even know how I would begin to make that happen. I'd have to get back down there and find a place to stay," I responded.

"We'll pay for the flight. You can stay with us," she said.

That warm feeling welled up within my chest again. I thought to myself that the Lord was closing doors only to open this one. What an adventure this was going to be! Sure enough, the very next day I was back in Los Angeles, California. Every early morning was regimented with my dedications in the Lord involving prayer and scripture study followed by getting our granddaughter to her school in Bel Air. After getting Alina to school, we would then proceed to get Elva to her job at Paramount Pictures. Then Wanda would take me all over the Los Angeles area to different restaurants for breakfast. She also showed me where her "ward" was. At the time, I didn't understand the meaning of the word, but she explained to me that it was her church, and that is what they called them: wards.

■ ■ ■ ■ ■ ■ ■

Wanda's mom had always been a Christian, and their family had believed in God and worshiped Him growing up. They attended a Union Baptist Church, but one day in Wanda's adulthood, her family was talking about their church experience, and they all agreed that it seemed something was missing. They decided that they were going to go to different churches to see if they could find one where they could feel whatever it was that was missing. After visiting each of the different churches, they would sit and talk in the parking lot about their experiences. Invariably, they were left saying, "It was good, but it's not quite right."

They did this for two years. Eventually, Wanda's mom moved to Simi Valley, California. One day the missionaries knocked on her door. She invited them in, and they taught her about the gospel. Incredibly, perhaps as a result of some divine orchestration, the missionaries knocked on Wanda's door the very same day in an entirely different city—and Wanda's mom hadn't sent them. The Lord was working to bring this family to Him, even though they now lived many miles apart.

In that first meeting, the missionaries said three words that changed Wanda's heart and life forever: "God loves you." She had never really known that before, and it seemed to be exactly what her soul needed to fill that missing piece in her worship experience. As the missionaries continued teaching her about the plan of salvation, she found that there were now answers to all the questions she had carried for so long.

Wanda was soon baptized, as were her mom, dad, and two daughters. They decided they were going to live together. They moved to the Canoga Park Ward in Los Angeles. The missionaries came out and blessed their new homes, and Wanda felt that she had never before been so secure in the decisions she was making in her life. All of the things she had ever been concerned about were now resolved. She was so overjoyed by the blessings of the Church in her life that she tried to share the good news of the gospel with anybody who would listen! She especially wanted to let Black Americans know that they didn't have to struggle—that they didn't have to live in pain and hardship, even though society had set life up that way for them. She wanted them to know that they have a Heavenly Father who loves them. She would often share the message that the enemy has put so many stones in our way, but we can overcome them through the Savior.

■ ■ ■ ■ ■ ■

One day after our regular routine, Wanda informed me that she wanted me to see her beautiful temple, and that we would visit the visitors' center. There was a gold figure on top of this great majestic building. I would later find out that this was the angel named Moroni. I was in awe of not only the building but of the pristine surroundings as well. I asked Wanda if we were going inside this temple, and she informed me that only members of her church were allowed in. When she escorted me into the visitors' center, she began to show me all the different portraits of people who had once lived on the face of the earth and followed the teachings of Jesus Christ. There were names of people I had never heard before. They were not the same names I was accustomed to hearing about in the Bible. They were strange names. One in particular was Nephi.

"Are you trying to convert me to your religion?" I asked Wanda.

"No, I just want you to know what I'm about," she replied.

I didn't understand how these people could have such a connection with Jesus Christ when I hadn't heard of any of them.

Then, I was taken aback for a moment when I saw a familiar picture of what looked to be twelve bulls with a large bowl on their backs. Wanda said it was a baptismal font. I recalled something I'd seen a picture of many years before. I remember I was seventeen years old. It was a time when I didn't spend much time at home, because I had gotten a little wild and hard to handle. Daddy was ready for me to take my behavior elsewhere. But, one day, my mother got in touch with me and wanted to show me something. This was around 1964. When I arrived home, she was all excited about some tour she had been on at some temple in the Oakland hills. In the glossy brochures was the same baptismal font. At the visitors' center, Wanda explained that the animals were oxen, and they represented the twelve tribes of Israel.

Years after my mother shared that brochure with me, when we were young adults, Wanda and I were enchanted by the Oakland temple along the 580 freeway. We decided to look at this beautiful marvel up close. When we arrived, we were in awe of the entire estate. We proceeded to the front door. As it opened, we were received by a gentleman all in white, who informed us that we could not enter. He told us that to enter, we had to be Church members. It was quite a letdown, as we had wanted to satisfy the mystery of what this place was about.

I was grateful that Wanda was willing to share this part of her life with me now and that she had learned the answers to some of our questions about those beautiful buildings. I had no understanding of what was before me, but I was glad that she had expressed to me that all of this was important to her. I was also grateful that she had shown me where her ward building was, because this allowed me to have a place where I could pay my tithing. On any given day, I would put money into an envelope and go to her ward and drop it in the mail slot. Wanda found out what I was doing when I asked her to drive by her church one night. Upon doing so, I asked her to pull over. I went to the mail slot, dropped the envelope inside, and returned to the car. When she realized what I was doing, she seemed to think it was humorous.

"Sweetheart, why don't you at least put your name on the envelope?" she asked.

"God knows who is giving it," I replied. Wanda and I laughed.

I came to see that among the ways the Lord **26**
was guiding my life, He had also reunited me
with my childhood sweetheart. Those nights on
the phone, Wanda and I had talked about each wanting to be
married. Neither of us had ever married anyone. But we hadn't
come right out and said that we wanted to marry each other.

When Wanda and I originally split up in our youth, we
had been immature in our relationship. Yes, we always had a
nice place to stay and had nice things, but we had never been
schooled in communication and positive relationships. In that
time, it wasn't common for adults to prepare kids for serious
relationships. So there had been a lot of nonsense in our behavior toward each other—pettiness, egos, selfishness, and the
like—that got in the way of having a successful partnership.
Fortunately, all of those things that had caused us to split up
in the first place no longer existed in us when we came back
together. We had both grown and matured in important ways,
and it was now easy for us to let go of any petty arguments or
silly conflicts. Our transitions by way of Jesus Christ made these

issues so insignificant. Now, with clearness of heart and mind, Wanda and I decided that we would be married.

We had already agreed to keep ourselves pure so that the Lord would honor our marriage. After our wedding, we went on a honeymoon cruise to the Mexican Riviera. Elva and Alina came along also. We had a wonderful time, and it was time that I needed with them as a family.

Wanda would often make the statement that she wanted to be sealed to me for time and eternity. "Sure! No problem," I would always respond. Early on, I didn't know what that entailed. I later found out that it was something that needed to take place in God's holy temple, which I was not qualified for as of yet.

∎ ∎ ∎ ∎ ∎ ∎ ∎

Oftentimes during my morning dedication to the Lord, I would ask in fervent prayer that He would lead me to where He would have me worship. I knew—or at least I felt I knew—that God didn't want me to continually worship alone, for how could I learn all that I needed to on my own? Another important part of my prayers would be that the Lord would lead me to others who were like-minded.

Wanda and Elva knew what kind of church I was accustomed to and decided that I would have a good experience at a church located in South Central Los Angeles, which had become a megachurch. The format of teaching, preaching, and singing was very similar to that of my much smaller church in Oakland. The church was quite jovial. Everyone seemed to have a wonderful time. I know I enjoyed the teaching, the preaching, and the music. The church was very popular. Many celebrities could be found at this church any given Sunday, such as Earvin "Magic" Johnson, Denzel Washington, Stevie Wonder, or Angela Bassett. I would notice that after the pastor would get everybody lathered up, he'd have everyone all over the auditorium-style chapel form a humongous line leading into another area. There, they would sign some sort of contractual agreement. This agreement involved declaring what their salary was and then agreeing to pay ten percent of that salary to this church. Needless to say, I would never get into this line, for it felt like people were being herded like cattle off to the slaughter and being taken advantage of in their elevated state.

It was very kind of Wanda and Elva to try to help me in this way, but after several visits to that megachurch, I felt change was needed. The next Sunday morning, I began to ponder the idea of learning more about the church I was already paying tithes to. So, I decided that Sunday morning that I would go to my family's church with them. From the time we entered the parking lot, I observed that many of the parishioners at my family's church were white. When I saw some Asians and a few Hispanics, I realized that this would not be a traditional experience. Even though I was a stranger, I was greeted as though I were a friend. At the megachurch, I had been spoken to only one time by another member. I noticed slight smiles on Wanda's and Elva's faces, as if they knew something I didn't. A multitude of white members greeted my family with hugs and kisses and smiles. One white-haired man named Jack seemed to adore my granddaughter. I was told that even in her infancy, he would always hold her in his lap during the meeting they called sacrament. Members greeted me with handshakes and smiles while looking me straight in the eyes. I looked them back in the eyes. My mother had always told me to look others in the eye.

However, this time, I did not see what I was so accustomed to seeing in the eyes of white people. These people did not just pretend they saw me when they really didn't. Here, something was different, but it was too much for me to understand at the moment.

In the holy sanctuary, I felt a sense of peace that came over the entire room as young men recited beautiful words concerning our Savior. It seemed so powerful and loving. My eyes filled with tears and my heart with gratitude that I was being allowed to take part in all of this. This way of worship was not anything I understood or had known before. I only knew in my heart that it was right.

I felt that I could have sat in the sanctuary for hours, but before I knew it, the meeting was over. After a song and prayer, everyone began to stand and head for the rear of the chapel. Some went out of the doors on the right, and some went to the left. I didn't know which way to go. I looked to my family and asked, "Where do I go? Do I follow you?"

Wanda and Elva escorted me to the rear of the sanctuary toward a gentleman who was seated on the very last row. "Ed, this is our friend Bob Petersen," Wanda said. Bob seemed especially glad to meet me because he was a dear friend of both my wife and my sister-in-law. I believe he was glad to hear that Wanda had gotten married! "Ed, go with Bob," they said. "He'll take care of you."

■ ■ ■ ■ ■ ■ ■

I had learned over the years that whites could indeed be friends with Blacks. Some even became friends with me— in fact, I was quite popular with my friends of all ethnicities.

However, I had never been in a situation in church where a white man was to take the lead and I was to follow. All of this was new and, I have to admit, somewhat exciting. We entered a classroom setting for Sunday School, and it was so energetic with so much enthusiastic participation that I wanted to participate as well. Because of my Bible studies, the Lord had given me some understanding of the scriptures, so I could be involved.

What really touched me was the next class, which consisted of all men. They called it the high priests quorum. At the time, I did not understand the meaning of this quorum, but I witnessed that these men carried a wonderful and mighty spirit. They taught about the deeper things of God and His kingdom. Often, I had to remind myself to close my mouth—it kept falling wide open in amazement.

After being born again, I had read through the Bible a couple of times. Many years later, I read it a few more. Many times, though, I would read the Bible and have no idea what certain passages meant. For example, as mentioned before, I had no clue about the temple, the priesthood, premortal existence, garments, or other amazing things referred to in both the Old and New Testaments. Sitting in on these new church meetings provided me with a new understanding. Teachers and students alike would often make reference to a book they called "another testament of Jesus Christ"—in other words, the Book of Mormon. I then realized that this book contained the stories of Nephi and the other people I had seen in the temple visitors' center.

I must have been squirming in my chair in high priests quorum. Bob leaned over and said, "Go ahead, Ed. Go ahead and speak—you're allowed to. We want you to."

So, I began participating as well. What great joy it was, and how exciting it was to learn of the mysteries of God. How exciting it was to discuss things I had never heard of or addressed in my early years. Every week, someone was visiting our home from the church. Oftentimes I would hear different titles that I didn't understand. I'd hear of home teachers, visiting teachers, or missionaries. Sometimes people would visit and they didn't have a title at all. They were just friends of my family from the church.

Two men called missionaries would visit the **27** house at the same time each week. I would take that opportunity to go upstairs and watch some sports. However, one day my wife informed me that the missionaries had inquired about how I would feel about them visiting me. "You would have to ask him," my wife and sister-in-law replied. I didn't really know what to think of this, because I really didn't understand the missionaries' role in the workings of things.

One evening, I received a phone call. I was still a stranger in a strange land. Who could be calling me? Could it be my sister, or could it be one of my daughters? No—it was the missionaries! They were requesting to come and visit me. This brought delight to my heart, because I immediately remembered my prayer to be able to associate with men who were like-minded. After a brief conversation with a missionary named Elder MacLeod, I believed this was an answer from on high. An appointment was made, and I was very excited but also anxious for that day. I knew from our conversation that we were going to be speaking on the gospel of Jesus Christ. I was prepared with a pencil, a pen, a notebook, a copy of the King James Bible, and a copy of the New International Version of the Bible. I was ready to study and discover the word of God. The missionaries brought Bob Petersen with them. Upon their arrival, my whole family cleared the entire space. I was surprised, but I didn't question it.

We had a wonderful time in scripture, and then they began to teach me about the Book of Mormon. They also taught me about Joseph Smith, a prophet. They told me about Joseph Smith's conversion as a young boy in a grove of trees. There, Heavenly Father and Jesus Christ appeared to him. He had been in turmoil, as he wanted to find out which denomination of Christianity was correct. I learned that Joseph was instructed by God to follow His Son, and not any of the churches that existed at the time. During several more visits, the missionaries shared many other things pertaining to the Book of Mormon, the story of Joseph Smith, and the doctrine of The Church of Jesus Christ of Latter-day Saints.

I recalled how the Church was rejected by other Christians, namely the ones that I had been affiliated with during my born-again time in Hawaii. Those people had called the Church a cult, even not knowing any details about it. I wondered to myself how such a spirit of the Lord could loom so large in a religion if it wasn't true. One night, while I was studying the Book of Mormon and jotting down notes in my notebook, the light-bulb came on in my mind. It made all the sense in the world that The Church of Jesus Christ of Latter-day Saints would be persecuted and even rejected by other Christian organizations, because Jesus was at the forefront of this Church. Why wouldn't it be attacked by those who didn't know the entire truth of all things? That gave me the assurance that I didn't really need to understand everything right away. If Jesus was at the head of the Church, that was enough. Because of how God had led and taught me, I knew the Church was true. I didn't need further proof than that.

■ ■ ■ ■ ■ ■ ■

I never mentioned my love for jazz to anyone in the Church. My family, of course, already knew. Oddly enough, the missionaries started to bring an elder statesman-type with the name Jack Cohen to our visits. He was an accomplished jazz trumpet player who at the time played locally in the Los Angeles area. Needless to say, we clicked right away and became very good friends. One night, after a study session with Jack and the missionaries, Elder Rehr said that all Church members needed to follow the Word of Wisdom. He explained that Church members are not to use drugs, alcohol, coffee, or caffeinated tea. That gave me the opportunity to say playfully that the Lord had set me up. Yes, He had set me up so that I would already be prepared to embrace the Church of Jesus Christ fully. I told the missionaries the story of how the Lord had removed all of the aforementioned entrapments from me before I had even come to church for the first time. They all received my story with the humor it deserved.

But then, one of the missionaries explained to me that after learning about the Church, people are offered the opportunity to be baptized. I reflected on what one of the cofounders of a men's Christian organization in West Oakland had preached. He said that once people are baptized, they never have to be baptized again. The elder explained to me that a baptism must be done by someone who has the proper authority. I thought about the many self-proclaimed preachers from the neighborhoods I grew up in. I understood where the elder was coming from. So, I joyfully agreed to be baptized.

After everyone left, I went upstairs, put away my books, and read through my notes. I knew that I was going to have to tell my wife and my sister-in-law the decision I had made. They had never made any comments about my studies or my meetings with the missionaries. The most they would ask was an occasional, "How did the lesson go?" They never tried to influence or pressure my decision to join the Church. I called them upstairs and asked them to be seated.

"I have made a sound decision to become baptized into The Church of Jesus Christ of Latter-day Saints," I said to them. Both my wife and my sister-in-law broke out in tears. My own eyes began to well up full of water, but they were tears of joy. I was about to be baptized by someone who had the authority to do so. Amen.

My baptism was scheduled for August 12, 2006—almost a year after my first visit to Los Angeles. I wasn't sure what to expect. I thought back to my first experience with baptism, which had been somewhat frightening. I hadn't understood a thing about what was happening to me, and I wasn't told why it was necessary. My baptism in Kaimuki, Hawaii, was the second one. That time, I knew I needed redemption, and I knew I needed help. However, there were still so many things within me that I was not ready to give up and turn over to the Lord.

The third time was the charm. My wife, sister-in-law, and granddaughter were there to watch me get baptized. To my surprise, there were many ward members there as well. My good friend Bob Petersen had agreed to perform the baptism. There was a bit of irony involved in this, as Bob worked in the gang division of the Los Angeles Police Department. Indeed, God does have a sense of humor.

After the baptism, I had a feeling of freshness and newness. I had great anticipation for what the Lord had in store for me next. It was a joyful gathering of well wishes, hugs, and handshakes. The look of delight in my wife's and family's eyes was more than enough to assure me that I was definitely on the right path.

Jesus Christ admonished us to love our fellow man. The Lord meant that we must show love toward every living being on the face of the earth, irrespective of what race, creed, or color they are. Even though I had not been raised to be racist against whites, nearly everything I had seen or heard about white people was negative. All that I had seen on TV pertaining to whites showed them hanging Black people in the South, or burning our churches down, or sicking dogs on my people for wanting to vote. But all whites weren't the same!

Needless to say, many of my fears from childhood had been calmed. Instead of judging others by their race, I began to see others based on their actions and behavior. I realized I had been operating in the same mode as those who were racist and would stereotype me or my people.

Through fasting, learning in the Church, and prayer, I began to be spiritually convicted of important issues deep within my heart—namely, loving my fellow man. This does not mean only being socially polite, but loving others in the way that Jesus means for us to do. The scriptures tell us that you cannot love God if you do not love your fellow man. The scriptures also tell us that the Lord chastens those whom He loves. I knew that the work that needed to be done on my innermost self would be difficult. Over the years, I had developed some serious trust issues, yet I knew I had faith. I considered these trust issues, among other issues, to be bondages. I knew that my strength was going to have to come from the Lord according to my faith. From the time that the Lord first touched me that night I cried out to Him, my heart had begun to soften toward so many people and things from my past. I also discovered that there were many things I had to forgive myself for.

I began to have compassion for others. I knew that these feelings could only be due to the influence of the gospel and the scriptures I'd studied throughout my journey. Many times, I have had to repent or ask the Lord for forgiveness. During these times, I have found out once again that we have a benevolent God full of love, mercy, and grace.

■ ■ ■ ■ ■ ■ ■

While still in my early days of being a Church member, Wanda advised me that I should receive my patriarchal blessing. At the time, I had no idea what that was. She then told me that every stake in the Church has a patriarch. In a prayer, he gives you your lineage in the house of Israel and inspired personal counsel or direction from the Lord, including promises and warnings. Early on in our marriage, I remember waking up around two or three in the morning. I saw Wanda working feverishly on the computer. The next morning, I asked her what she had been doing. She was working on genealogy. I asked her what the genealogy was for, and she simply replied, "Our ancestors." At the time, I thought it was kind of futile for her to do that, since we came from slaves. She paid no attention to what I was saying, and the very next morning, she was at it again.

As it turned out, the patriarch would say something significant regarding genealogy to me during my blessing. First, he told me what tribe of Israel I was part of. Second, he told me that if I did the work of my ancestors in the temple of the Lord, then the Lord would bless me with being able to provide for my family. This had always been a deep concern of mine, and the Lord seemed to be aware of it.

Once I joined the Church, my wife had begun to share the joys of the temple. I knew that if I was going to do the work of my ancestors, I would need to learn what the temple was all about. Wanda had received her endowment and participated in sacred ordinances there, and she had a firm testimony of the blessings that came from temple worship. Bob Petersen had also shared his testimony of the temple with me, and he ended up becoming my temple prep teacher. Bob and Wanda focused less on the specifics of what the temple was and more on how attending the temple made them feel.

I was already in awe at the idea of being a member of God's priesthood. I felt a specialness about holding that authority from God to do His work on earth, but now I was going to make more covenants and receive blessings for my eternity. When I went to the temple to receive my endowment, I felt that I was being set on a hill, separated from a lot of the ills in life. This temple experience made me feel that in spite of whatever happened in this life, I was going to be okay in eternity. I felt that from that point on, everything I did was going to be an investment in my eternity, all because of my endowment. It was a humbling experience but a very wonderful one.

When I received my endowment, I could see the joyous look in my wife's eyes, my sister-in-law's eyes, and my friends' eyes who were there with me as brothers. I knew that I didn't have the full understanding of the great event that had just taken place, but I felt I was truly an heir of the Lord. I felt special— not better than anyone, but of value. Worth. Power. I felt confidence. I felt that now I was going to be living life so much more differently than before. I was going through the stages to be purified and sanctified. The work toward that sanctification began when I went to the temple for the first time, and it continues still as I return there to worship and learn again and again.

After Wanda and I were sealed, I reflected on the recurring dream I'd had throughout my life in which I lived happily with a loving family in a Spirit-filled home. It finally all fit and all made sense. The Holy Ghost had been giving me glimpses of where I was going to end up.

■ ■ ■ ■ ■ ■ ■

I was so overjoyed about being a member of The Church of Jesus Christ of Latter-day Saints. I felt I had arrived to a level of happiness in life that I hadn't known existed. To be close to God wasn't just an idea, and to be a friend of God wasn't just a concept. It was a reality, a lifestyle, a way of being, and my participation in the relationship could determine my closeness. My belief, faith, trust, and hope dictated my spiritual future. I finally knew with all surety that the living God, a living Savior, and a Holy Spirit all love and care about each of us. It isn't a concept—it's the truth. It's something you feel, and it's with you on a daily basis. Whether you are good or bad, happy or sad, God is with you through it all and will never forsake you.

I even came to realize that being a member of the Church has the ability to elevate your thinking and improve your character and your personality, because all of your efforts are blessed and strengthened beyond your own capacity through the Holy Ghost. You can even love more deeply as a follower of Jesus Christ. I could say to my wife, "I love you," and I would mean it, but I have come to learn by the Holy Spirit that the more I love God and Jesus Christ, the more I can love my wife. I can even love strangers more sincerely. That increase of knowledge and wisdom through the Holy Ghost never stops—the Spirit always elevates our thoughts and understanding.

People of African descent have always had to **29** consider racial issues in their lives. Racial issues exist in every field: social, economic, financial, emotional, political, and religious. In the realm of Christianity, none of this should be a stumbling block against how one should behave as a brother or sister in Christ. Christ is the operative word—the living word. Christ's example shows us how we can have liberty, peace, love, and kindness toward others. Christ's example also teaches us generosity, humility, and other virtues that quench the issues I've already mentioned. These issues take the oxygen from humanity, yet Christ replenishes it.

Many brothers and sisters who are white may feel that they do not need to concern themselves with racial issues. It is a luxury to have the option to ignore important topics that affect others. However, it is also a disadvantage to oneself to choose not to be in harmony with everyone. No one should put his or her head in the sand, including Black people. If we all ignore the problem, then nothing gets solved—including within Christianity. Christ being in one's life starts the transition to solve all differences, for He is the answer.

One day, I wanted to share something that I had written

with another member of the Church. He was a friend and brother in Christ whom I loved and respected. Much of what I had written was a commentary on race and how racial issues have affected the Black community negatively throughout history. I could see and sense disdain in him as I read out portions of my piece. I decided to stop sooner than I had planned and asked for comments and critiques. My friend began to express how sick he was of hearing how badly white people had historically treated Black people. "After all, *I* wasn't part of the whites who enslaved Blacks," he said. He believed that because he wasn't part of the atrocities of the past, he didn't have any responsibility to the present. He couldn't see (or chose not to see) that some of the social, economic, and even environmental structures in place exist due to investing in or voting toward the status quo. He could not see that he was also implicit, whether by choice or by complacency. I had only shared this piece of writing with him to get an opinion on the delivery and flow of the message. It had not been my intention to make him uncomfortable, but he was. "Aren't things better now?" he asked. I simply told him yes. In that moment, I felt that our friendship was more important than trying to teach him about race.

One of the things that had attracted me to The Church of Jesus Christ of Latter-day Saints was the multi-ethnic look of each congregation. Though it was still predominately white, in my own experience, those I came in contact with did not seem to care about the color of my skin or the fact that I am of African descent. I know that is not the experience of all Black members, but I look forward to the day when it can be.

■ ■ ■ ■ ■ ■ ■

The baggage of race still found me in the Church. It found me one night at the kitchen table with my wife and sister-in-law. They were expressing their joy that I had received the Aaronic Priesthood. Wanda mentioned that she knew that I would honor the priesthood. Of course I would! I had been satisfied with just becoming a member of the Church. When I found out about the priesthood and its origin and that I could become a priesthood holder, I was in awe. I often expressed my spiritual wonder to Wanda, who enlightened me about the history of Blacks in the Church.

Wanda shared that she was so excited when she joined The Church of Jesus Christ of Latter-day Saints that she wanted to tell everyone she had found the answer. Wanda hoped all of her family and friends could experience the joy she had found in the Church of Jesus Christ. Her two daughters, Traci and Jinga, were baptized. Wanda's mother, Sylvia, and sister, Elva, also joined the Church. Wanda and Elva's friends Calvin and Dolores joined. Wanda's brother Ronnie and his wife joined.

On the day of Wanda's aunt and uncle's baptism, the bishop stood at the pulpit to address the members with a story. This story, however, was insensitive. He said that he was dreaming about walking down a long road. During this walk, he saw a truck approaching full of watermelons. The truck rolled over, and all of the watermelons went flying! The bishop yelled, in an exaggerated voice, "Oh, Lord! Please don't let them overtake me!!" His dream made a mockery of all the Black sons and daughters of God who were joining His Church. This was very painful for Wanda, as she had brought so many new Black members to the Church. Wanda knew how valuable being a part of the Church could be for her people, but her own bishop had told an embarrassing, racist joke.

Wanda received a great deal of love and support from members of the Church, but unfortunately, she also experienced painful instances of racism in other members' words and actions. Whether it was demeaning statements about Black people in Sunday School or a woman in the temple refusing to be helped by Wanda and asking for a white temple worker instead, cruel offenses have come her way many times. Most Black members of the Church could share their own stories of racism and insensitivity at the hands of white members. It is sad but also understandable that some turn away from the Church when they are treated by other members as unwelcome and less than.

Even Wanda, with her deep love for God and for Jesus Christ, went through a period of struggles with the Church after experiencing harsh racism from her bishop and other Church leadership.

During the next two years, she started going to other churches here and there. It was a painful time in her life, because things got bad for her economically as well. It was during this time that Wanda and her sister Elva started living together.

One morning Wanda was sitting on the couch when something said to her, "You need to go back to church."

She replied, "I'm not going back."

"Why?" the voice asked her.

"They're racist bigots, and I don't want to have to deal with them," she answered.

Just then Wanda's sister entered the room and asked, "Who are you talking to?" Wanda could not deny that she had heard the voice and promptings of the Spirit instructing her to go back to church, despite the flaws of its members, and so she agreed to go. Upon her return, a woman in her ward, also named Wanda, walked up to her and said, "We really need you here. Thank you so much for coming. We love you." That was just the loving welcome she needed to remind her why she was truly there and for the negativity to fly out the window. Despite everything that had happened, she knew that her Heavenly Father is at the head of this gospel, along with Jesus Christ, and that They love us all. They have a wonderful plan of salvation for us, and she needed to continue sharing it with everyone she could.

■ ■ ■ ■ ■ ■ ■

Wanda's sister Elva had found great joy in the Church as well, only to be discouraged during a conversation she had with a bishop one day. She had just expressed how she was looking forward to being sealed in the temple of the Lord. The bishop's response was, "Elva, you would have to be with *your* people to do that."

Elva knew that the Church was predominately white, but she still asked him, "What do you mean?"

The bishop informed her that she had to be with "her kind" in order to be sealed in the temple. He was preaching the false notion that people should marry only those from their own race, which unfortunately has been a belief held by many people both inside and outside of the Church. Until that moment, Elva had felt that she *was* with her kind—brothers and sisters in Christ. That unwelcoming comment caused her to leave the Church for around a year and a half.

Wanda and Elva both later expressed their regret for letting others' ignorance cause them to lose valuable time in the Church. But in time, they told me more. Wanda and my sister-in-law informed me that people of African descent were not able to have temple access and that the priesthood was not accessible to worthy males of all races until 1978. On June 1, 1978, President Spencer W. Kimball had received the revelation that *all* worthy men could receive the priesthood. But after learning this, I seriously looked into the matter and found out that there was no record or declaration that any revelation had been received by the First Presidency of the Church teaching that people of African descent could *not* have temple access. Furthermore, there was no record or official declaration from the First Presidency saying that Black men could not hold the priesthood. The more I discovered, the more I desired to learn about the history of my people in God's Church.

Both Wanda and I have had times of needing to remember what the core of the gospel is all about and to focus on that, because inevitably, the next offensive or ignorant remark will come. Despite that, we know we want to live with our Heavenly Father for eternity. We want to be with Him, and that should be everybody's goal. He promised us that if we do the things He says, we can return to Him. We may not feel worthy or feel like we can do it, but He can sanctify us and perfect us if we are willing to trust in Him. And so we continue on with eternity as our goal, even when it is difficult.

I don't remember the chain of events that happened that caused us to have the opportunity to meet a very interesting and well-informed **30** member of the Church named Marvin Perkins, who happened to be a Black man. Brother Perkins visited us in our home. While engaged in conversation about the Church, the subject of race came up. With that, Marvin began to expound on the history of Blacks who had held the priesthood in The Church of Jesus Christ of Latter-day Saints in the 1800s. You could have knocked us all over with a feather. We had already become aware of Marvin's work with a Black Church member and journalist by the name Darius Gray, because a friend had given us a DVD called *Blacks in the Scriptures*. Marvin was coauthor of this film, along with Darius Gray. We found out later that Darius Gray was coauthor with Margaret Blair Young of *Standing on the Promises*, a book series about the experiences of early African American members of the Church. So, we felt that what Marvin told us was certainly legitimate and true.

The Lord was moving in our lives in a mighty way. Wanda, Elva, and I met the Relief Society president of our new stake. She also happened to be Black. Her name was Alma Bailey. My wife immediately took the opportunity to invite her over for dinner. During dinner, Alma mentioned the historical material of *Standing on the Promises* and offered to let me borrow the books. After reading them, I discovered new worlds of information concerning Black Saints in the Church of Jesus Christ in the 1800s—Saints like Elijah Abel, one of the first African American members of the Church, who was ordained to the priesthood in 1836.

After a few weeks, we received a call from Sister Bailey informing us that she was going to be released as Relief Society president and would be put in place as a chairman for the African-American Public Relations Counsel in The Church of Jesus Christ of Latter-day Saints. She was excited, and she let us know that she wanted us to be a part of it as well. With Alma's visits to our home, she had learned a lot about our stories and felt that our testimonies could be used by the Lord to minister to others. We were set apart by the stake president, and the work began.

Alma decided that for her first event, she would advertise "Panther to Priesthood," where I would share my experience in the Black Panther Party and how my life had ultimately led to my conversion to the gospel. When the night arrived, it was standing room only. In fact, after Wanda and I spoke, there was a line of people that led all the way out of the church building. They wanted to meet us and get to know us. Even though there were refreshments, Wanda and I didn't get a chance to have anything to eat! By the time we were finished, the cleanup crew was putting everything away. Regardless, we felt an overwhelming joy for what the Lord had allowed us to be a part of. Many talks followed after that, all over the western United States. It was especially meaningful to speak at my old stomping grounds in Oakland, California—specifically, at the Oakland temple. Two of my old buddies attended. One of them is now a member of the Church.

As we became more informed about Blacks in the Church through our affiliation with the African-American Public Relations Counsel, we began to share what we were learning with others. Often in the middle of my speaking engagements, I would notice many white members' jaws drop upon hearing that Blacks had held the priesthood in the 1800s. It was my thinking that even though many of the members in the audience were covenant children who had been born into the Church, they and their families had no idea that Black pioneers had existed. Of course, many Black people—members and non-members alike—were unaware as well. Most did not have access to information about Black pioneers. But faithful Latter-day Saints like Marvin Perkins and Darius Gray were working hard to share the message that Blacks were not only present in the early Church, but prominent, contributing members.

Elijah Abel, a Black man, was baptized in 1832 and received the priesthood in 1836. Abel was ordained into the Third Quorum of the Seventy in Kirtland, Ohio, in December 1836 and participated in the construction, dedication, and early ordinances of the Kirtland Temple. Joseph T. Ball, another American of African descent, was also baptized in 1832. He went on a mission to New England and New Jersey with Wilford Woodruff. It was recorded in Brother Woodruff's journal that Brother Ball was an elder, having received the priesthood. Walker Lewis was baptized by Parley P. Pratt in the 1840s and ordained to the priesthood by William Smith. These are just a few examples of the many men and women who were dedicated Black members and pioneers. There are treasure troves to be learned about people like Green Flake, Jane Manning James, Elizabeth Flake Rowan, Oscar Crosby, Nettie James Leggroan, and countless others. I have to admit that discovering the roots of Black people in The Church of Jesus Christ of Latter-day Saints was precious to my family and me. That sense of community, of belonging, and of purpose that I had sought in various places my entire life was now all coming together in the Lord's way.

■ ■ ■ ■ ■ ■ ■

A few months after Spencer W. Kimball had proclaimed the revelation that all worthy men could receive the priesthood, my wife, Wanda, was helping Brit McConkie, Elder Bruce R. McConkie's brother, to encourage the Church to reach out to people of other faiths. Brit McConkie was the president of the Los Angeles temple. Wanda and Brother McConkie decided to reach out to the Black Baptist ministers of the Southern California convention, which had many ministers, preachers, and pastors. There was a constant outreach by Brother McConkie and Wanda, but most of the Baptist leaders refused their efforts.

There was one exception, and that was Reverend Rufus. Reverend Rufus was befriended by Brother McConkie and Wanda. Through that friendship, Rufus was able to witness the Christlike spirit of two members of our Church. He was also shown much love and charity from Brother McConkie, and that was enough for him to listen to the message of the gospel. He became convinced of its truth through the Spirit, and along with his wife, children, some extended family, and nearly twenty of his parishioners, he was baptized.

There are many African Americans who often point out the time in the Church's history that Black people were not allowed the privilege of entering the Lord's holy temple, or the period when Black men were unable to hold the priesthood of the Lord. Many will use this as a tool to speak against the Church and as a reason not to join. Though it is valid to feel hurt or confused by some things in the Church's past, as I think of all of the obstacles, racism, and discrimination that my ancestors—brothers and sisters of African descent—have overcome, I realize that we should not allow human error to keep us from the riches of Christ. Reverend Rufus and his family and congregation would not allow others' ignorance to keep them from a better life through what the Church had to offer in Christ, both spiritually and temporally.

. . . .

Over time, I realized through personal revelation that my attempts to feel value in life would never succeed if they were determined only by the feelings and behaviors of man. I could not get liberty, freedom, or purpose from any man—whether Black or white. No political or philosophical group could give me what I needed deep inside. I discovered that only Christ Jesus could fulfill what was needed to wash away the burdens that were self-inflicted or systematically placed on and in my life—and to make me whole. I have truly found freedom and liberty through Christ Jesus, and the Lord steered me toward The Church of Jesus Christ of Latter-day Saints so that I could receive these monumental blessings.

However, I am not naïve. I know there are people in this Church who still have racist ideas and uphold racist practices. I also know that none of us who carry, live by, and practice this hate will go without having to face the Lord and answer for why one hated their brother, sister, or neighbor based on the color of their skin. "All are alike unto God," the Book of Mormon teaches (2 Nephi 26:33). Jesus came for all of us, not just some.

From the time I joined the Church, the Lord **31** has kept me busy. I was first a substitute Sunday School teacher. The regular Sunday School teacher was a businessman, and his work required a lot of travel. A substitute teacher was needed. The regular teacher told me that he'd had a dream that I should be his substitute! So I accepted, even though my knees were quivering at the thought of being a substitute teacher. At the time, the Church was ending their year studying the New Testament, and we were then in the book of Revelation. In the past, this book had often scared me. This time, it became a book of love. I learned a lot. From there, I gained the Aaronic Priesthood and then the Melchizedek Priesthood. I began to administer the sacrament. Later on, I became the first counselor in the Sunday School, and then Sunday School president—twice! I served on the high council. Most recently, I have served as a Primary teacher.

Over the course of sixteen years and three different wards, I have never felt more loved than I have in The Church of Jesus Christ of Latter-day Saints. I had sought belonging and answers in so many places, from school to the Black Panthers to music groups and more, but I found them completely as a member of this Church. My experience in the Church is only one of millions. There are Relief Society and priesthood quorum members who are constantly serving the Lord for the sake of others all over the world. There are Saints of all races, creeds, and colors. Yes, it is unfortunate, and even terrible, that my wife, sister-in-law, and other members of African descent have had to feel the sting of racism in the Church. You could likely find a racist in any church—but that doesn't change our purpose for being there. We're there to learn to love, to serve Christ, to serve our fellow man, and most importantly, to gain salvation. Human beings of all kinds need deliverance from the trials and temptations that would keep us from loving one another and ourselves. If we keep our eye on the Lord, we will get the help we need to become better. If we remain faithful, there is a promise of eternity, which is incomparable to anything on this earth. Man will disappoint you, but God is faithful. He loves us yesterday, today, and forever. No matter how strong a man or woman might seem, they can never outdo the love, power, and purpose that the Almighty God has for you. Whether you're white, Black, Native American, Asian, Latino, or any other race, if God is with you, then no one can stand against you.

I am not fully sanctified yet, and I know that I will continue to make mistakes through this lifelong process. The enemy will continue to put trials and temptations before me. But God is faithful, and He will have the victory. He has my plan in His hands, and as long as I am confident in that, then I am striving for perfection in Jesus Christ.

It is my testimony that God is alive and at the forefront of this Church, His Church, and He moves His Church in a holy way. If you are willing to experience the transforming power of God through His Church, you too can have your life made full, no matter how difficult or complicated your path has been. My life is a testimony to that truth. The Lord has done exactly what the patriarch said He would do for me. He has blessed me and my family abundantly. I'm so thankful that through all the struggle of my life and my quest to understand who I am and why I am here, He has always had an eternal plan for me. He has one for all of us.

ACKNOWLEDGMENTS

I'd like to give thanks to my wife, Wanda, for her belief in what this manuscript can do to lead people to Christ; Elva Clay, my sister-in-law, for her encouragement; my granddaughter Alina Johnson for her help with good grammar; President Michael Payne for that every-now-and-then kick in the pants to keep going with the book; and Russell Stevenson for his kindness and professionalism.